Illustrator
Ken Tunell

Editorial Manager
Ina Massler Levin, M.A.

Editor-in-Chief
Sharon Coan, M.S. Ed.

Creative Director
Elayne Roberts

Art Coordinator
Denice Adorno

Cover Artist
Larry Bauer

Product Manager
Phil Garcia

Imaging
Ralph Olmedo, Jr.
James Edward Grace

Researcher
Christine Johnson

Publishers
Rachelle Cracchiolo, M.S. Ed.
Mary Dupuy Smith, M.S. Ed.

The Eighties

Author

Dona Herweck Rice

Teacher Created Materials, Inc.
6421 Industry Way
Westminster, CA 92683
www.teachercreated.com
ISBN-1-57690-030-4
©2000 Teacher Created Materials, Inc.
Reprinted, 2004
Made in U.S.A.

Table of Contents

Table of Contents *(cont.)*

Introduction

The 20th Century is a series which examines the political, economic, social, cultural, scientific, and technological advances of the twentieth century and introduces students to individuals who made history in each decade.

The Eighties chronicles American and international life during the ninth decade of the century, a time filled with as much optimism as anarchy, as much prosperity as poverty. Governmental structures that had been systematically built through war and revolution were beginning to tumble in the face of growing resistance and international cries for change. National boundaries blurred as individual countries joined in economic links that would begin to connect the world. Restrictions that had managed and restrained businesses unleashed their holds. At the same time, attempts were made to confine the cultural awareness that had permeated the cultural revolution of the sixties and seventies. American politics and politicians attempted to bring back America's glory days, a sense of "Main Street U.S.A." as seen through rose-colored glasses, while voices around the world declared that oppression, tyranny, and poverty were still in full force, even in America.

During the 1980s, Americans enjoyed tremendous technological advances and a strong economy. They also experienced a breakdown in the ability to live with simple comforts, and they were likewise harnessed with a far-reaching recession. Enormous advances were made in matters of health and longevity, while at the same time a frightening and deadly disease began to spread like wildfire. Its very name created fear and suspicions and brought forward long-held prejudices in some while others opened their hearts in love and acceptance.

The eighties saw tremendous advancements for women. Sandra Day O'Connor became the first female American Supreme Court Justice, Margaret Thatcher held fast as Prime Minister of Great Britain, and Geraldine Ferraro became the first female American candidate for vice president on a major party ticket. Yet even while these strides were being made, women around the world continued to earn wages far less than men for the very same jobs; also, women continued to bear the majority of the burden of home and family care, despite the fact that many of them were working full-time outside the home.

While studying the eighties, you will find a variety of aids in this unit to help make your studies complete, including the following:

- **a time line**—a chronology of significant events of the decade
- **planning guides**—summaries and suggestions for introducing the issues and events of the decade
- **personality profiles**—brief biographies of important individuals of the decade
- **world views**—chronology and details of world events of the decade
- **language experience ideas**—suggestions for writing and vocabulary building
- **group activities**—assignments to foster cooperative learning
- **topics for further research**—suggestions for extending the unit
- **literature connections**—summaries of related books and suggested activities for expanding them
- **curriculum connections**—activities in math, art, language arts, social studies, and music
- **computer applications**—suggestions for selecting and using software to supplement this unit
- **bibliography**—suggestions for additional resources on the decade

To keep this valuable resource intact so that it can be used year after year, you may wish to punch holes in the pages and store them in a three-ring binder.

Time Line

	1980	1981
Politics and Economics	UN General Assembly calls for Soviet troops to withdraw from Afghanistan. Pierre Trudeau regains his office as Prime Minister of Canada. The U.S. attempt to free the hostages held at the U.S. Embassy in Iran fails with tragic results. Zimbabwe, formerly Rhodesia, gains independence and elects its first Prime Minister. Ronald Reagan is elected U.S. President in a landslide victory over the incumbent, Jimmy Carter. Republicans control the Senate for the first time since 1964.	Coinciding with the inauguration of Ronald Reagan, Iranian terrorists release all 52 hostages. President Reagan's proposed budget introduces the largest tax and spending cuts to date. John Hinckley shoots President Reagan, James Brady (the White House Press Secretary), and two others outside a Washington, D.C. hotel. Secretary of State Alexander Haig mistakenly declares that he is in charge of the nation. Former Vice President Spiro Agnew is convicted of taking bribes. The first national conference of Solidarity, a worker's union, is held in Poland. Egyptian President Anwar el-Sadat is assassinated by soldiers while attending a military parade. Sandra Day O'Connor becomes the first female U.S. Supreme Court Justice.
Social and Cultural	The Olympic Games in Moscow are boycotted by over 50 nations protesting the Soviet invasion of Afghanistan. Mary Decker becomes the first woman to run a mile in less than 4.5 minutes. John Lennon is shot and killed outside a New York hotel. *Dallas* mania sweeps the U.S. as 88.6 million viewers, the most ever to watch a single television program, tune in to learn "who shot J.R." Terry Fox of Canada runs the Marathon of Hope to raise funds for cancer research. Ann Meyers becomes the first woman to try out for the NBA; she does not make the team, however. Bjorn Borg of Sweden wins his fifth successive Wimbledon title.	Pope John Paul II is shot in St. Peter's Square. He fully recovers. The musical *Cats* is first performed in London. It becomes an enormous but surprising success. South Africans get their second television channel, this one aimed at the black population. Prince Charles and Lady Diana Spencer are married in St. Paul's Cathedral, London. Over 12,000 air traffic controllers strike in the U.S. and are dismissed from their jobs.
Science and Technology	Mt. St. Helens in Washington erupts, shooting debris twelve miles high. 57 people die. A severe heat wave throughout the southern U.S. results in more than 1,000 deaths. The World Health Organization formally announces the eradication of smallpox. The remains of the *Titanic* are found in the North Atlantic, over 12,000 feet below the surface. The space probe *Voyager 1* takes photos of Saturn and its rings. Six new moons are spotted.	The first U.S. space shuttle successfully completes its maiden flight. Acquired Immune Deficiency Syndrome (AIDS) is first identified. IBM introduces its personal computer (PC). Skull surgery is successfully performed on an unborn baby by University of Denver surgeons. Chinese scientists are the first to successfully clone a fish.

Time Line *(cont.)*

1982	1983	1984
The U.K. and Argentina go to war in the Falkland Islands. Britain is victorious.	Strategic Arms Reduction Talks take place in Geneva. Both the US and USSR, leading offenders, are responsive.	Yuri Andropov of the Soviet Union dies; Konstantin Chernenko is his successor.
Canada breaks its last legal ties with Britain.	Reagan proposes the Strategic Defense Initiative (nicknamed "Star Wars") to be used against the "Evil Empire," the USSR.	Pierre Trudeau resigns as Canada's Prime Minister.
The Polish Parliament votes to ban Solidarity.		Geraldine Ferraro becomes the first U.S. woman to run for vice president on a major party ticket.
Leonid Brezhnev of the Soviet Union dies and is succeeded by Yuri Andropov.	Reagan backs the Contra rebels in Nicaragua.	Indian Prime Minister Indira Gandhi is assassinated by her Sikh bodyguards.
	Drought and famine wrack Ethiopia. The nation calls for world relief.	More than seventy U.S. banks fail, the highest number since 1937.
	Benigno Aquino, frontrunner against President Marcos of the Philippines, is assassinated at the Manila airport.	
	US unemployment is the highest since 1941.	
The Vietnam Veterans War Memorial is dedicated in Washington, D.C.	Reagan signs legislation to make Martin Luther King Jr. Day a national holiday, beginning in 1986.	The PG–13 film rating is instituted.
The newspaper *U.S.A. Today* is first published.		Band Aid, under the direction of rocker Bob Geldoff, releases "Do They Know It's Christmas?" recorded to provide financial relief to Ethiopians struck with famine.
John Paul II becomes the first pope to visit the United Kingdom.	Lech Walesa, a leader in the Solidarity movement of Poland, is awarded the Nobel Peace Prize.	Singer Michael Jackson wins an unprecedented eight Grammy Awards for his album *Thriller.*
Sun Myung Moon, leader of the Unification Church (Moonies), marries more than 2,000 couples in a mass wedding at Madison Square Garden. Moon matches the couples himself.	Guion Bluford becomes the first black astronaut. Sally Ride is the first American woman in space.	The USSR and other communist nations boycott the Olympic Games in Los Angeles in retaliation for the 1980 boycott in Moscow.
Grace Kelly, Princess of Monaco, dies in a car crash.		Seven U.S. chemical companies agree to pay 15,000 Vietnam veterans affected by "Agent Orange" 180 million dollars.
The U.S. Department of Justice ends bans on the frequency and length of television commercials.		
After a lengthy antitrust suit, "Ma Bell" sells two-thirds of its holdings.	*Pioneer 10* is the first spacecraft to leave the solar system after eleven years in flight.	The Apple Macintosh computer is introduced.
Dutch Elm disease kills twenty million trees in the United Kingdom.	Compact disc players hit the market.	American astronauts become the first to fly untethered in space.
The first color photos of Venus are taken by a Soviet space probe.	The world land speed record is set by Richard Noble of Britain, who reached 633.6 mph.	The AIDS virus is discovered simultaneously in the U.S. and France.
An American surgical team implants the first permanent artificial heart in a human patient. The patient, Barney Clark, dies of complications 112 days later.		"Baby Fae" receives a baboon heart transplant. She lives for twenty days.
		The genetic difference between chimpanzees and humans is discovered to be less than one percent.

Time Line *(cont.)*

1985	1986	1987
Daniel Ortega becomes president of Nicaragua. Chernenko of the Soviet Union dies. Mikhail Gorbachev is his successor. Wilma Mankiller becomes the first female principal chief of the Cherokee Nation. Gorbachev halts all deployment of medium range missiles in Europe. A TWA airplane is highjacked by Arab terrorists. The US makes sanctions against South Africa in protest of apartheid. An Italian cruise ship is highjacked by Palestinian terrorists. Gorbachev and Reagan meet in Geneva for a two-day summit.	Corazón Aquino, widow of Benigno, becomes the Philippine President. Marcos flees the nation. Olof Palme, the Swedish Prime Minister, is assassinated by an unknown gunman. The shooting shocks that nation renowned for its pacifism. Europe instigates sanctions against South Africa. Pressure on the nation mounts. The "Irangate" scandal rocks the US as the government admits to secret arms deals with Iran. Insider trading scandals make headlines.	Gorbachev's campaign for *glasnost* and *perestroika* (openness and reconstruction) leads to major changes in the USSR. Reagan and Gorbachev sign a treaty banning all short and medium-range nuclear weapons from Germany. In a televised Congressional hearing, the US government is accused of providing $40 million to Nicaraguan Contra rebels. The stockmarket crashes on Black Monday; while the Dow Jones Index falls 508 points.
"We Are the World" is recorded by U.S.A. for Africa to benefit Ethiopia. The band is comprised of many popular American recording artists of the time. The Live Aid rock concert raises more than sixty million dollars for famine relief in Africa. Pete Rose breaks Ty Cobb's career base hits record with 4,192 hits. Cobb's record had stood since 1928.	Pope John Paul II leads one hundred international religious leaders in prayers for peace. More than one hundred years after it was begun, the *Oxford English Dictionary* publishes its last volume (Se–Z). Greg Lemond is the first American to win the Tour de France. Prince Andrew and Sarah Ferguson of Britain are married. Four nuclear reactors at the power plant in Chernobyl, Ukraine, suddenly malfunction, causing many deaths and injuries, and some destruction. The effects are felt around the world.	Evangelist Jim Bakker resigns under allegations of adultery. Senator Gary Hart, a frontrunner in the Democratic campaign for the presidency, withdraws from the election under similar allegations. Baby M's surrogate mother draws national attention while seeking custody. She loses the case. Bill Gates, the founder of Microsoft, becomes the first billionaire of the microcomputer industry. The world's five-billionth inhabitant is born (in Yugoslavia).
A hole in the ozone layer over Antarctica is discovered. Lasers are used surgically to clear blocked arteries. University of California, Berkeley, scientists gather evidence of a black hole at the galaxy's center.	The space shuttle *Challenger* explodes just after takeoff, killing all seven passengers, including the first civilian in space, Christa McAuliffe. *Voyager* becomes the first aircraft to fly non-stop without refueling around the planet. It takes pilots Jeanna Yeager and Dick Rutan nine days to complete the journey. Controversy surrounds the colorization of old black-and-white films. *Voyager 2* discovers ten new moons of Uranus. The first triple transplant (heart, lung, and liver) is performed by British surgeons.	One second is deleted from the year to adjust it to the Gregorian calendar. A South African woman is implanted with her daughter's fertilized ova. She gives birth to her own grandchildren. Russian cosmonaut Yuri Romanenko comes back to earth after a record 326 days in space at the Mir space station.

Time Line *(cont.)*

	Politics and Economics	Social and Cultural	Science and Technology
1989	Emperor Hirohito of Japan dies after reigning since 1926. Pro-democracy Chinese students in Tiananmen Square, Beijing, demonstrate for seven weeks. Eventually the government brings in military tanks to disperse them, killing hundreds, if not thousands. Solidarity wins in Polish Parliament elections in an overwhelming landslide. Lt. Col. Oliver North is found guilty in the Iran-Contra scandal. The Berlin Wall comes down after 28 years, and free travel to the West is sanctioned. The Romanian government is overthrown. President Ceausescu and his wife are executed. Three hundred billion dollars are allocated by the U.S. government to save the nation's savings and loan industry.	Author Salman Rushdie goes into hiding after Muslims issue a *fatwa* (death sentence) over the publication of his book *The Satanic Verses.* General Colin Powell becomes the first black American to be named Chairman of the Joint Chiefs of Staff. Evangelist Jim Bakker is convicted of fraud and sentenced to forty-five years in prison. The world's largest entertainment group is created when Time Inc. purchases Warner Communications for thirteen billion dollars. Baseball legend Pete Rose is banned from the sport after allegedly gambling on the games.	Eleven million gallons of oil spill off the coast of Alaska as the *Exxon Valdez* runs aground. A gas pipeline explosion in the Trans-Siberian Railroad kills four hundred people. The *Voyager 2* space probe reaches Neptune, the farthest planet from the sun at the time. DNA "fingerprinting" is used as evidence in criminal cases for the first time. The largest known prime number is discovered by U.S. mathematicians. It has 65,087 digits.
1988	General Manuel Noriega of Panama is indicted in the U.S. on charges of drug smuggling. Polish Solidarity strikes are rampant, causing the government to talk directly with Lech Walesa. Soviet troops begin to leave Afghanistan after a nine-year occupation. One million South African blacks strike in protest against labor laws. Ethnic Albanians in Kosovo, Yugoslavia, demonstrate for freedom from Serbian rule.	Use of crack, a cocaine derivative, is on the rise throughout the U.S. The McDonald's restaurant chain opens facilities in Moscow. Smoking is banned on all U.S. flights of under two hours. A terrorist bomb in Pan Am flight 103 kills 270 people over Scotland. Steffi Graf of West Germany becomes only the fifth tennis player to win the Grand Slam.	A massive fire burns nearly 90,000 acres in Yellowstone National Park. A tidal wave in Bangladesh kills 3,000 people; an earthquake in Armenia kills 80,000. Brain cell transplants are performed for the first time. The B-2 "Stealth" bomber of the United States is shown for the first time. The Shroud of Turin, carbon dated to 1330 A.D., is disproved as the burial cloth of Jesus. Taking aspirin daily is shown to cut the risk of heart attack in half. *Discovery* is the first successful manned space shuttle launch since the *Challenger* tragedy.

Using the Time Line

Use pages five to eight to create a visual display for your classroom. Follow the steps outlined below to assemble the time line as a bulletin board, and then choose from the suggested uses those that best suit your classroom needs.

Bulletin Board Assembly

Copy pages five to eight. Enlarge and/or color them, if desired. Tape the pages together to form a continuous time line, and attach it to a prepared bulletin board background or a classroom wall. (To make a reusable bulletin board, glue each page of the time line to oaktag. After the glue has dried, laminate the pages. Write on the laminated pages with dry-erase markers.)

	1980	1981	1982	1983	1984	1985	1986	1987	1988	1989	
Politics and Economics											**Politics and Economics**
Social and Cultural											**Social and Cultural**
Science and Technology											**Science and Technology**

Suggested Uses

1. Use the time line to assess students' initial knowledge of the era. Construct a web to find out what they know about the Berlin Wall or the space shuttle Challenger, for example. Find out what they would like to know. Plan your lessons accordingly.

2. Assign each group of students a specific year. As they research that year, let them add pictures, names, and events to the appropriate area of the time line.

3. Ask students to discover what other events were happening around the world during the ninth decade of the twentieth century. Tell them to add that information to the bottom of the time line.

4. After adding new names, places, and events to the time line, use the information gathered as a study guide for assessment. Base your quizzes and exams on those people, places, and events which you have studied.

5. After the time line has been on display for a few days, begin to quiz students about the people, places, and events named there. Call on one student at a time to stand so that he or she is facing away from the actual time line. Ask a question based on the information. Variation: Let the students compose the questions.

6. Use the time line as a springboard for a class discussion; for example, who was the most famous or influential person of the ninth decade? How have the inventions of that time affected their lives today? How was life in those years similar to or different from their lives today?

7. Divide the students into three groups and assign each group a different area: politics/economics, society/culture, and science/technology. Have each group brainstorm important related people, places, and events that lived or occurred during the ninth decade. Then create a group mural depicting these important happenings and people. Get permission to paint a hallway, or tape several sheets of butcher paper together to make a giant canvas.

8. Assign groups of students to make specialized time lines—for example, a time line of events leading to the eventual breakdown of the Soviet Union (in the nineties) or the release of the hostages from Iran (in the early eighties).

Eighties Overview

- President Jimmy Carter leaves the presidency. On his last day in office, American hostages in Iran are finally released after more than a year in captivity. The release dovetails with the inauguration of President Ronald Reagan.

- Pope John Paul II is shot, but he recovers and gains the admiration of the world by forgiving his attacker. President Ronald Reagan is also shot, and he, too, recovers. A third victim, Indira Gandhi, Prime Minister of India, is shot and killed by her bodyguards.

- Rock musician John Lennon is shot and killed in front of the New York hotel at which he is staying. Millions of fans grieve his sudden death.

- Britain and Argentina go to war over the Falkland Islands. The United States invades Panama and Grenada and bombs Libyan terrorist bases. Israel forces the PLO from Lebanon. Iran and Iraq go to war. Russia continues its invasion of Afghanistan for nearly a decade.

- A new military defense strategy called "Star Wars" gains momentum. The world superpowers agree to reduce nuclear missiles.

- Famine in Ethiopia kills millions. Many make great efforts to relieve the famine, most notably rock musician Bob Geldof and his concert called Live Aid, which earns millions for relief.

- Mikhail Gorbachev comes to power in the USSR, bringing about a push toward democracy.

- A nuclear power reactor explodes in Chernobyl, USSR, killing and wounding thousands. The effects of the blast are far-reaching.

- Chinese students in Tiananmen Square protest the government in China. Many are killed by government soldiers who squelch the uprising.

- The Soviet Union begins to unravel, and numerous Soviet bloc countries overthrow communism. The Berlin Wall comes down, and East and West Germany are unified.

- The world's stock markets crash. Insider trading scandals rock the financial world.

- Congress holds hearings over the Iran-Contra affair, uncovering a secret arms deal with American antagonist Iran. Marine Lieutenant Colonel Oliver North admits to secretly funneling money to the Contras, an army of Nicaraguan rebels.

- Sandra Day O'Connor becomes the first female American Supreme Court Justice. Sally Ride becomes the first American woman in space. Elizabeth Dole becomes the first woman to head the U.S. Department of Transportation. Geraldine Ferraro becomes the first female candidate on a major party ticket for the office of vice president.

- Technology revolutionizes the American home with personal computers, VCRs, compact disc players, and more.

- Terrorism around the world is on the rise with a number of highjackings, bombings, and hostage situations, most for political reasons.

- A battle against apartheid continues in South Africa and around the world.

- Corazón Aquino is elected Philippine president, replacing President Ferdinand Marcos who is implicated in the murder of Aquino's husband, a former presidential hopeful.

- Human Immunodeficiency Virus (HIV), a retrovirus, is discovered to be the cause of Acquired Immune Deficiency Syndrome (AIDS). The first permanent artificial heart is placed in a patient.

Introducing the Eighties

On this page you will find some interesting ways to introduce the eighties to the students. Keep in mind that these are suggestions only, and it is not necessary to use all of them. Your project selections should be based on student needs, interests, and objectives.

1. **Music:** Learn about popular songs and musical styles of the decade, including new wave, punk, power pop, heavy metal, rap, and dance music (an extension of disco). Your local music store will have collections of pop songs from the period. Be sure, however, to listen carefully to the lyrics before playing them for your students, as some are likely to be offensive or controversial.

2. **Fashion:** Everything from preppie styles to punk were in vogue during the decade. Thrift stores are sure to have clothing from the period, and the students' parents are likely to have a few items as well. Begin your study of the period with an eighties fashion show or dress-up party. (Note: Music videos from the time are an excellent source for fashion ideas. Cable music channels still show videos from the decade as part of their regular airplay.)

3. **Artwork:** Display artwork either of the time or that reflects the time. Artists to investigate include David Hockney, Andy Warhol, Christo Javacheff, and architectural designer I.M. Pei. Assign students to create their own artwork or designs that reflect the decade and its great artists.

4. **Shoes:** Shoe fashions vary with each passing decade. Some popular styles in the eighties include penny loafers, Doc Marten combat-style boots, designer athletic shoes, high-top tennis shoes, and low-cut boots. Find pictures or actual samples of shoes from the time period. Make a classroom display. Include information about the different lifestyles that may have corresponded to the various types of footwear.

5. **Guest Speaker:** Contact local colleges, universities, museums, and historic societies for potential speakers who are experts on the era. Of course, there are countless individuals who have direct and first-hand memories of the decade who may also be expert speakers (particularly those who were involved in significant events of the time). Be sure to have students prepare questions ahead of time to ask the speaker.

6. **Interview:** Allow students to dress as famous people from the decade and, having researched their roles, to answer questions for the class as the figures might have done in a contemporary interview.

7. **Technology:** Technology boomed during the eighties, particularly in the area of computers. Research some of these technological advancements and the life-changing effects they had on society. Suggested items to study include the personal home computer, the compact disc player, the video player and recorder, and the video camera.

8. **Exercise:** Fitness boomed during the eighties. Jane Fonda's workout videos became some of the biggest sellers of the time, and energetic and dynamic fitness gurus came to the forefront in all types of exercise regimes. The video market greatly enhanced the workout craze. Take a look at some of these early workout videos. Follow some of them as part of your physical education program.

Discussing the Eighties

Create student interest with a lively discussion. Suggested topics and some methods for implementing them follow.

Terrorism: Acts of terrorism were not uncommon throughout the decade. Various terrorist organizations routinely took hostages, bombed buildings, and hijacked planes and boats. Discuss some of these events, the groups behind them, and how effective their actions proved in the end.

Communism: The breakdown of communism began during the eighties. Look at the events of the decade that began to wear away the communist structure. Discuss how and why communism began to erode. Also discuss other forms of government, including dictatorships, monarchies, democracies, and republics, among others.

Wall Street: The economy was a source of big business, big loss, and big crime throughout the decade. Discuss how Wall Street operates and how such things as insider trading and failed institutions affect the overall economic health of the nation and the world.

Rainbow Coalition: The Rainbow Coalition was a term utilized by presidential hopeful Rev. Jesse Jackson during the eighties. Discuss the Rainbow Coalition, what it meant to Jackson, and whether or not the students feel such a philosophy could be played out in reality.

Equal Rights Amendment: The push for the passage of the Equal Rights Amendment ended during the eighties, although it has been consistently reintroduced at the opening session of each new Congress. However, despite its failure, many individual states went on to pass their own equality-for-the-sexes laws. Discuss the amendment and whether or not the students think it is a viable and worthwhile one. Why do they think it failed? Do they believe it might pass at another time?

Environmentalism: A sense of urgency concerning the environment became palpable during the eighties. Such disasters as Chernobyl and the *Exxon-Valdez* oil spill resulted in various legislative pushes and grass-roots operations to improve the world's declining ecological systems. Discuss these movements, their effectiveness, and how ecology has improved or worsened since the eighties.

AIDS: One of the most frightening terms of the eighties was a four-letter acronym: AIDS. Confusion and panic surrounding the debilitating disease spread quickly through a frightened world. As scientists scrambled to uncover its cause and to find a cure, the number of individuals stricken with and dying of the disease leapt dramatically with each passing year. Discuss the effect that AIDS had on society during the eighties. Compare its effects to those of polio earlier in the century. Also discuss the advancements made in understanding and treating the disease.

Entertainment: Certain individuals in the entertainment industry became celebrities of phenomenal proportions during the eighties. Among the "big name, big money" celebrities were Michael Jackson, Bill Cosby, Madonna, and Whitney Houston. Discuss the concept of "celebrity" and the astronomical dollars that often come with the territory.

Soviet Invasion of Afghanistan

In December of 1979, the Soviet Union began sending thousands of troops into Afghanistan. This military intervention was in support of the Marxist Afghan government, which was threatened by growing unrest among the people of Afghanistan.

In reaction to the Soviet invasion, opposition to the government became a national resistance movement. The *mujahideen* (Islamic warriors) were poorly equipped but relentless in their defense and attacks. Using guerilla tactics, they persisted for several years. The Soviets and Kabul government retaliated by bombing villages at will, but the mujahideen—although outnumbered and out-powered—could not be stopped.

Nations around the world ardently criticized Soviet actions. President Carter of the United States stopped delivery of seventeen million metric tons of grain that was to be transported to the Soviet Union. Considering the Soviet actions a "serious threat to peace," Carter imposed a limited trade embargo and cut back the availability of American waters for Soviets to fish. In addition, all cultural and economic trades were cancelled. Finally, Carter pressured the U.S. Olympic Committee to withdraw from the Summer Games to be held in Moscow in 1980.

The Soviets called Carter "wicked and malicious." They declared that they were not, in fact, invading Afghanistan, but rather they were supporting the Kabul government there. Carter believed, however, that the Soviet presence in Afghanistan would pose a serious threat to Iran and Pakistan. Throughout the occupation, the United States did not let up on its protests.

A United Nations resolution in 1986 called for a negotiated settlement of the war. In 1987, an international Islamic conference asked the Soviet Union to withdraw from Afghanistan, and the Kabul government announced plans for a cease-fire. The resistance forces rejected the cease-fire. Later that year, a nationwide gathering of tribal leaders approved a new constitution and elected Sayid Mohammed Najibullah president.

Finally, in April of 1988, accords were reached which established a timetable for Soviet withdrawal. The accords were signed by Afghanistan, Russia, Pakistan, and the United States, but not by the politically divided mujahideen. The mujahideen continued to fight, attacking Russian troops as they left the country. The United States and the Soviet Union agreed in 1991 to stop giving military aid to the warring factions. In April of 1992, the resistance finally succeeded in overthrowing the Kabul government. Factions of the mujahideen agreed to a transitional government; however, fighting continued among the factions themselves as they each competed for power in the new government.

Suggested Activities

Cartography: Draw maps of Afghanistan, Russia, Pakistan, and Iran, showing their relationships to one another.

For Thought: Consider and discuss why the U.S. was so opposed to the invasion, since the Soviets were working with the Afghanistan government.

New Administration: Research to find out how the Reagan administration felt about the Soviet occupation of Afghanistan. Did Reagan agree with Carter? What was his administration's relationship with the Soviet Union?

Hostages in Iran

Revolutionaries in Iran would come to have great significance to the lives of 52 Americans.

In the late 1970s, Iranian revolutionaries who opposed Shah Mohammad Reza Pahlavi banded together under Ayatollah Ruhollah Khomeini, a Muslim religious leader. Mass demonstrations, strikes, and riots broke out against the shah, and finally, in January of 1979, the shah left the country. Khomeini, who had been in exile in France, returned to Iran and established an Islamic republic.

The shah was allowed to enter the United States in November of 1979 for medical treatment. The new Iranian government demanded that he and the money he took with him be returned to Iran. However, President Jimmy Carter refused their demands.

Anti-American sentiment was high in the new government even before Carter's refusal. Because the United States had supported the shah, hatred of Americans was intense. In retaliation, a mob of 500 students invaded and seized the American Embassy in Teheran, Iran, on November 20, 1979. They took 66 hostages.

President Carter demanded their release. The terrorists refused, and Carter immediately froze all Iranian assets in the United States. The students declared that the hostages would be released only when the shah and the money were returned and the United States apologized for its role in supporting the shah. They then paraded the bound and blindfolded hostages before television cameras, chanting, "Death to America, death to Carter, death to the shah." They burned effigies of Carter and Uncle Sam, and they spat on, trampled, and burned the U.S. flag.

Mediators were sent to negotiate for the release of the hostages, but there was very little success. Thirteen hostages, primarily women and blacks, were released, leaving 53 hostages.

In April of 1980, the United States attempted a rescue mission. However, equipment broke down, the mission was aborted, and during the withdrawal a helicopter collided with a plane. Eight American servicemen were killed. The rescue mission was a drastic failure, and the Iranians cheered in the streets, declaring that they "had inflicted defeat and flight upon Americans."

In June of 1980, the shah died in Cairo; however, the terrorists refused to release the hostages. Days and months dragged on. Americans were shocked and grieved by the prolonged act of terrorism. Everywhere, people wore yellow ribbons and tied them to their cars as a show of support for the hostages and the acknowledgment that they would never rest until the prisoners were returned.

In November of 1980, President Carter lost the presidential election by a considerable margin. One factor leading to his defeat was his failure to obtain release of the hostages. Ironically, the hostages were finally released on the day of Ronald Reagan's inauguration. The date was January 20, 1981, and the hostages had spent a total of 444 days in captivity.

Suggested Activity

Up to Date: Learn about Iranian-American relations since 1981. How have they changed? What are the current conditions?

Star Wars

The 1980s saw Star Wars come to prominence, but Luke Skywalker was nowhere to be found. The term was used to describe a defense system proposed by President Ronald Reagan in 1983, six years after the movie of the same name was released. Reagan's Star Wars, the Strategic Defense Initiative (SDI), called for an antiballistic missile defense, using a system of ground- and space-based weapons technologies that could stop a first strike (initial nuclear attack) from the Soviet Union. The goal was to intercept and destroy incoming missiles high above the earth. Reagan said that he believed the new system would end the threat of a surprise nuclear attack. Others feared that the system could be used offensively.

Over the next few years, Reagan and General Secretary Mikhail Gorbachev of the Soviet Union participated in a series of summit meetings to negotiate a number of topics. In 1985, the summit opened with Gorbachev's call for an end to Star Wars and Reagan's adamant refusal. The two could come to no agreement on the issue.

In 1987, Reagan and Gorbachev did make some headway in the direction of nuclear disarmament. Following a serious breakdown in their talks, the two were able to come together again to sign the Intermediate Range Nuclear Forces Treaty, the first comprehensive nuclear arms control treaty. It called for the destruction of 1,500 Soviet and 350 American warheads. The destruction of these arms would result in a reduction of American-Soviet warheads by approximately four percent. The two nations also agreed to a series of checks on one another to verify that the treaty was being honored.

Negotiations for arms limitations continued under President George Bush. In 1991 the first Strategic Arms Reduction Treaty, START I, which called for a 25 percent reduction in warheads, was signed by Bush and Gorbachev. The dissolution of the Soviet Union in 1991 slowed START I's implementation, requiring separate treaties with former members of the USSR. START II, signed in January of 1993, provided for elimination of almost three-fourths of the nuclear warheads held by the signers over a nine-year period.

In 1993, President Bill Clinton formally ended SDI. In its place, the Ballistic Missile Defense Organization (BMDO), a land-based antimissile system, was established.

Suggested Activities

Science: Find out about nuclear weapons, how they work, and their potential for damage.

Debate: As a class, debate the efficacy of nuclear weapons. Some believe they are necessary for protection and as a deterrent. Others believe that their lethal power makes them inhumane and unacceptable.

Cold War: The term Cold War first came into being in the 1940s. Find out about the history of the term.

SALT and START: Research to learn more about the Strategic Arms Limitation Talks (SALT) of the 1970s and the Strategic Arms Reduction Treaties (START I and II) of 1991 and 1993.

Iran-Contra Scandal

The American people were shocked in the mid-eighties to learn of a secret arms deal with Iran, a Middle Eastern country and United States antagonist. United States policy expressly forbade the trading of arms for the release of hostages; however, the American people learned that the administration under Ronald Reagan secretly sold missiles and missile components to Iran. United States hostages held by terrorists were released as a result of the sale. Moreover, profits from the illegal sale of arms were used to provide aid to the Contras, a band of rebels in Nicaragua. The Reagan administration supported the Contra efforts against the Sandinistas, but Congress stopped financial support in 1983. Illegal support continued, however, through the sale of the missiles.

Oliver North

At the forefront of the support to the Contras was a Marine lieutenant colonel named Oliver North, a member of the U.S. National Security Council. North told Congress, in a televised hearing in 1987, that he did indeed deliver financial aid to the Contras, but North also said that he acted only at the command of his superiors and that he always believed President Reagan was fully aware of his actions.

The public became torn over the issue of Oliver North. Some believed that the government was using him as a scapegoat to keep blame from themselves. Others saw him as a hero, doing the work he was trained to do in good faith. Others in the government were implicated, and two were forced to resign. The National Security Council Chief Vice Admiral John Poindexter resigned his post, as did Donald Regan, White House Chief of Staff. Throughout it all, Ronald Reagan adamantly denied any knowledge of the missile sale and exchange or the aid to the Contras. For the most part, he was believed by the American people; however, Reagan's reputation in office was never quite the same.

Oliver North was convicted in a federal court on three charges in the Iran-Contra affair. Poindexter was convicted of conspiracy and of lying to Congress during the investigation; however, his conviction was overturned in appeals court. In 1992, President George Bush pardoned several others who had been involved, including Caspar W. Weinberger, Reagan's Secretary of Defense.

Suggested Activities

Research and Compare: Find out about another scandal (for example, Watergate in the Nixon administration or Whitewater under President Clinton). How did it affect the American public? Report to the class on what you find.

Nicaragua and Iran: Learn about the nations of Nicaragua and Iran since the mid-eighties. What became of the Contra rebels and the Sandinista government?

After the Hearings: Research to find what happened to Oliver North after the congressional hearings.

Discussion: Hold a class discussion about the issues involved in the Iran-Contra hearings, such as the exchange of weapons for hostages and government aid to foreign rebel forces.

Insider Trading

A star of Wall Street, the financial wizard Michael Milken, took a huge fall in 1989. Throughout most of the eighties, he had been a celebrity of sorts, earning $550 million a year and more than a billion dollars by the time he was forty years old. Yet, in 1989, he was facing a $600 million fine and ten years in jail.

The 1980s were a time of economic struggle for millions; but for some Wall Street wizards like Michael Milken, they were a financial paradise. Milken was a Wall Street bond trader who knew how to play the market effectively. He was a junk-bond king, and his economic prowess saw him at the inception of the cable industry, the cellular industry, Ted Turner's broadcasting empire, and more. His bonds even made it possible for MCI's "David" to compete with AT&T's "Goliath." It seemed there was nothing this young wizard could not foresee, and certainly there was no way of stopping him from turning his vision to gold.

Michael Milken

What a crash it was when, in 1989, Milken was charged with 98 counts of racketeering and securities fraud. At first, Milken maintained his innocence; however, he eventually cut a deal with the federal government. He pled guilty to some charges in exchange for others being dropped. His sentence was ten years in prison and $600 million in fines.

In the eighties, Milken had been a symbol of success, the American dream at its best. Countless young people followed his lead, briefcase in hand, using their ambition and drive to climb the ladder of success. Milken's fall was quite a wake-up call, and it and other events seemed to turn the tide of the "Greedy Eighties." The following decade saw a societal shift toward family values instead of the single life of the young urban professional ("Yuppies" as they came to be called) fighting for a piece of the pie. Milken's fall had far-reaching effects, for himself and society as a whole.

Suggested Activities

Research: Research to learn about the life of Michael Milken since his conviction. He has been in the news on a somewhat consistent basis.

Economic Split: In the eighties, the world of the yuppie could be mirrored against millions of Americans living in poverty, many homeless and starving. Research to find out more about the conditions of the people who were not living the American dream. Discuss the relationship between the very rich and the very poor. Also discuss capitalism and its effects.

The Berlin Wall

On November 9, 1989, the Wall came tumbling down. Here is its history.

Following World War II, Germany was divided, creating West Germany and Soviet East Germany. Berlin, located inside East Germany, was also divided into East and West zones. In the late 1940s and through the 1950s, crossing from East Berlin to West Berlin in Germany became a popular way to escape Soviet communism. Thousands fled Soviet control in this way, and in 1961, more than one thousand East Germans were escaping each day. In order to stop the flight which drained the trained workforce of East Germany, East German police began to construct a wall on August 13, 1961. The wall was made of concrete topped with barbed wire. East Germans continued to escape after the wall was built, but nearly two hundred died in the attempt. Border guards shot them on sight.

The wall became a symbol of the Iron Curtain, the military, political, and ideological barrier that existed between the Soviet bloc and Western Europe during the Cold War.

West Berlin itself was constantly under threat of having its supplies cut off. In 1971, Britain, France, and the Soviet Union reached an agreement that provided for free movement between West Berlin and West Germany. As the seventies and eighties progressed, relations between East and West Berlin began to improve.

In 1989, communist governments were failing and crowds of people were leaving East Germany through Hungary, Poland, and Czechoslovakia. People throughout East Germany were demanding freedom. In November of that year, the East German government succumbed, agreeing to free movement for its citizens. Consequently, the wall that had stood for nearly thirty years was opened. Thousands of people crossed the border within the first few hours of freedom. Citizens began to dismantle the wall any way they could, using picks and shovels and anything else available. People climbed the wall and danced on top, and tourists came from around the world to see the wall come down. Many took home small pieces of it as a reminder of the importance of freedom.

By the end of 1989, communism in East Germany was hanging by a thread. In October of 1990, East and West Germany became a single nation with Berlin as its capital. A few sections of the Berlin Wall are still standing and have become outdoor art galleries.

Suggested Activities

Airlift: In the late forties, West Berlin was cut off from its supply lines. Research to learn how long the seige lasted and what was done to support the people of West Berlin.

JFK: John Kennedy was president when the Wall was erected. During his visit to West Berlin in 1963, he spoke in German. Find out what he said and explain what it meant to the people of Berlin.

Cartography: Draw maps of Germany before and after the reunification.

Read: Read firsthand accounts of people who witnessed the tearing down of the Wall. Newspapers around the world carried the story for weeks.

Write: Write a story as though you are an East Berliner present on the day the Wall is opened.

Equal Rights Amendment

The Equal Rights Amendment (ERA) was legislation proposed in 1972 to amend the Constitution of the United States. The central message of the amendment stated that "equality of rights under the law shall not be denied or abridged by the United States or by any State on account of sex." If ratified, the ERA would have guaranteed that no law would allow rights to one sex and not to the other. Despite lobbying and debate, the ERA failed to be ratified ten years after its first passage in Congress.

The history of the ERA dates back to the early 20th century. In 1916, the National Woman's Party (NWP) was founded by suffragist Alice Paul. The party sought to establish equal rights under the law for women. Paul and others put their efforts into drafting and forwarding legislation at the state and federal levels that would guarantee equal rights. Strong opposition to their efforts arose in 1921 when former supporters argued that new laws would jeopardize other existing laws that were created to protect women from being exploited in the work force. Paul disagreed, stating that those laws that were meant to protect could also restrict women and keep them from employment opportunities.

In 1923, the NWP proposed an Equal Rights Amendment to the Constitution. To move forward, the law would require a two-thirds vote in both the Senate and the House of Representatives or a petition supported by two-thirds of the states' legislatures. If such a two-thirds marker were gained, then three-fourths of the states would need to ratify the amendment for it to become law. However, the proposal never earned the two-thirds majority.

The ERA was proposed to many ensuing Congresses, but each time it failed to get the two-thirds vote. Finally, in 1972, it earned the supporting vote in Congress and became ready for ratification by the states.

A growing body of women and women's organizations had been rallying around the ERA prior to 1972, particularly the National Organization for Women (NOW), founded in 1966. In a few years' time, NOW and others were able to gain a majority of support from both major political parties. In 1972, it also had the support of President Richard Nixon. It received the two-thirds vote and had the support of nearly every U.S. senator; clearly, the ERA had a growing momentum. However, opposition was also on the rise. Conservative organizations and political leaders expressed strident opposition, claiming that the ERA would hurt rather than help women. Phyllis Schlafly, a leading opponent to the amendment, declared that the ERA would tear down all female privileges as provided in their traditional roles. She and others also insisted that the ERA would prevent all restrictions on abortion. These arguments won over many legislators.

By June 1978, the ERA fell just two states short of the number needed for ratification. March 1979 was the date mandated by Congress as the deadline for complete ratification, but due to popular support, Congress allowed an extension. Lobbyists worked feverishly, but no additional state came forward to ratify the amendment. In May 1982, the ERA finally failed.

Following its failure, the ERA has consistently been resubmitted to Congress at each new session; however, it has yet to again receive the two-thirds majority vote. Despite this, by the century's close, sixteen individual states had allowed for equal rights within their own state constitutions.

Suggested Activity

Debate: Break into two groups to debate the pros and cons of the ERA.

Jesse Jackson

Born in Greenville, South Carolina, on October 8, 1941, Jesse Louis Burns took the name Jackson after his mother, who had delivered him while an unmarried teenager, married Charles Jackson. The Jackson family was poor, but young Jesse always felt their love and support.

While growing up in the South, Jackson was very aware of the disparity between black and white and the conditions in which they lived. All around him were signs that said "Whites Only." While good schools were nearby, Jackson had to walk five miles to an all-black school.

Jesse Jackson

The University of Illinois offered Jackson a football scholarship, and he accepted. However, he felt thwarted in his efforts to take an active role on campus, so he left Illinois to attend North Carolina Agricultural and Technical College, an all-black school. There he became a leader in the fight for civil rights. It was also there that he decided to take his faith in God and natural gift for public speaking and become a minister. After graduating from college, he enrolled at the Chicago Theological Seminary.

While joining in a civil rights march in Selma, Alabama, in 1965, Jackson met the leader, Martin Luther King, Jr. He decided to leave the seminary college to work under King, heading Operation Breadbasket in Chicago. He organized boycotts against white-owned businesses that did not hire blacks although they were in black neighborhoods. Jackson followed this work with the development of PUSH (People United to Serve Humanity). He also spent a great deal of time visiting young people in school, encouraging them and warning them against the use of drugs and teen pregnancy.

By the time the 1980s arrived, Jackson had a strong following and was a respected social leader and public speaker. In 1984, he decided to make a run for the presidency of the United States. He ran under the heading of the Rainbow Coalition, hoping that his platforms would appeal to people of all colors. He received 3.3 million votes in his bid for the Democratic nomination. Jackson ran again in 1988. He more than doubled his vote from the previous election, and in March of 1988, he took the Michigan primary. This was the first time in the history of the United States that a black person won a presidential primary election.

Jackson did not win the nomination or the presidency in either election, but he did break new ground by gaining the votes of people of all colors. He holds a distinguished place in the politics of the eighties.

Suggested Activities

Civil Rights: Jesse Jackson is one of many civil rights leaders of the twentieth century. Write a report on one such leader and present your findings to the class.

Since Then: Jackson has continued to be active in politics and social change. Read to find out more about his life since the 1988 election.

William Rehnquist

William Hubbs Rehnquist was born on October 1, 1924, in Milwaukee, Wisconsin. His father was an active Republican whose conservative views strongly influenced his son. Rehnquist's mother was a college graduate who spoke five languages and was an active community volunteer.

Rehnquist was bright and assertive as a child. When asked by a teacher what he wanted to do when he grew up, he responded, "I'm going to change the government." Rehnquist attended Kenyon College on a scholarship for one year, but left school in 1943 to join the Army Air Corps. The nation was currently at war, and Rehnquist wanted to do his part.

In 1945, Rehnquist attended Stanford University. Upon graduating, he went to Harvard graduate school for one year and then returned to Stanford to study law. He graduated at the top of his class in 1952. Upon graduating, he was asked by Judge Robert Houghwout Jackson to serve as his clerk in 1952–53. Very few new graduates are offered such an honor.

Rehnquist moved to Phoenix, Arizona, in 1953 to open a private law practice. It was at this time that his conservative views really began to show themselves. He spoke out in support of racial segregation in schools and the limitation of rights for criminals. He was strongly opposed to the views of Chief Justice Earl Warren, whom he considered a liberal. In 1964, Rehnquist campaigned for Barry Goldwater. Through this campaign, he gained a reputation as an influential spokesperson for the Republican Party. Such renown followed him, and in 1969, he was named Assistant U.S. Attorney General and head of the Office of Legal Counsel of the Department of Justice. He became a speaker throughout the nation, telling people about President Richard Nixon's programs and perspectives.

Richard Nixon appointed Rehnquist as an associate justice of the U.S. Supreme Court in 1971. Rehnquist officially took his seat in January 1972, and his conservative views were immediately evident. He urged for mass arrests of war protesters and for strident campaign reform. He became known as a Supreme Court dissenter. In 1973, he dissented from a decision to legalize abortion, and in 1976, he dissented from the decision that laws treating men and women differently should be legally examined. By 1986, Rehnquist had been the sole dissenter fifty-four times, far and away a record number.

When Chief Justice Warren Burger retired in 1986, President Ronald Reagan named Rehnquist as the 16th chief justice. Chief justices are rarely chosen from the ranks of the associate justices, and Rehnquist's appointment was strongly opposed by some because he was allegedly linked with several ultra-conservative organizations. However, after three months, the Senate confirmed his appointment.

The following two sessions of the Supreme Court remained moderate, but the 1988–89 session began to take a conservative swing. The Supreme Court decisions under Rehnquist have often been conservative and in support of judicial restraint.

Suggested Activities

Supreme Court: Learn about the function and history of the Supreme Court. Also consider how the politics of the various chief justices have affected Supreme Court decisions.

Conservative and Liberal: Learn about the meanings of the terms "conservative" and "liberal" as they are applied politically. Discuss the current political climate nationally and in your area.

James Earl Carter, Jr.

39th President, 1977–1981

Vice President: Walter F. Mondale

Born: October 1, 1924, in Plains, Georgia

Party: Democrat

Parents: James Carter, Lillian Gordy

First Lady: Eleanor Rosalynn Smith

Children: John, James Earl III, Jeffrey, Amy

Education: U.S. Naval Academy

Nickname: Hot

Famous Firsts:

- He was the first president to be born in a hospital.

- Jimmy Carter was the first president elected from the Deep South since before the Civil War.

Achievements:

- He served in the navy during World War II.

- After his father died, Jimmy Carter resigned from the navy, and he and his wife, Rosalynn, worked in the family's peanut-farming business.

- He was elected to the Senate in 1952.

- In the 1950s, Carter was the only white man in Plains, Georgia, who refused to join the White Citizens' Council, an organization supporting segregation.

- In 1966, he ran unsuccessfully for governor of Georgia. In 1970, he was elected governor.

- The Department of Energy and the Department of Education were created under his administration.

- He conducted the Camp David accords in 1978, bringing about peace between Israel and Egypt.

- President Carter pardoned the Vietnam draft evaders.

Interesting Facts:

- Carter was a speed-reader who could read over 2,000 words per minute with 95 percent accuracy.

- When he traveled, President Carter often carried his own luggage.

- Carter left office as one of the most unpopular presidents in history, yet he became one of the nation's most successful and active ex-presidents.

- His best remembered foreign relations event was the Iranian hostage crisis. After his final full day in office, the hostages were released.

- Jimmy Carter and his wife Rosalynn currently serve as regular volunteers for Habitat for Humanity, a program which develops and builds housing for low-income families.

Ronald Wilson Reagan

40th President, 1981–1989

Vice President: George Bush

Born: February 6, 1911, in Tampico, Illinois

Party: Republican

Parents: John Edward Reagan, Nelle Wilson

First Lady: Nancy Davis

Children: Maureen, Michael, Patricia, and Ronald

Education: Eureka College

Nickname: Dutch (given by his father)

Famous Firsts:

- Ronald Reagan was the first former film star to become president. He appeared in more than 50 feature films and several television shows.
- Reagan was the oldest man elected president. He was 69 at the time.
- He was the first to appoint a woman, Sandra Day O'Connor, to the Supreme Court. The post of secretary of transportation also went to a woman, Elizabeth H. Dole, for the first time.
- During Reagan's administration, the federal budget deficit reached a record level.
- In 1994, he became the first former president to publicly announce a personal battle with Alzheimer's disease.

Achievements:

- Reagan was a two-time California governor. He was also a longtime president of the Screen Actors Guild.
- In 1985, Reagan and Soviet General Secretary Mikhail Gorbachev agreed to unprecedented cultural, educational, and scientific exchanges between their nations.
- In 1987, Reagan signed a treaty with Gorbachev, reducing nuclear arms.
- The government under Reagan helped arrange for the removal of PLO units from Lebanon.
- He opened the Ronald Reagan Presidential Library in Simi Valley, California. It holds documents and other items related to his presidency.

Interesting Facts:

- American hostages held in Iran for more than a year were finally released on the day of Reagan's inauguration. They were on a plane out of Iran just minutes after he was inaugurated.
- In 1980, not only did Reagan win the election but the Republicans also took the majority in the Senate for the first time since 1952.
- There was an attempted assassination on Reagan in 1981. He was shot in the chest, but he fully recovered. In 1985, Reagan experienced another life-threatening battle, this time with colon cancer. He recovered rapidly again.
- His first job was as a lifeguard. He used money from that job and a partial scholarship to put himself through college. After college, he worked as a sports announcer.
- Reagan was initially a Democrat. In 1962, he became a Republican.
- Both of Reagan's presidential election victories were landslides.

George Herbert Walker Bush

41st President, 1989–1993

Vice President: J. Danforth (Dan) Quayle

Born: June 12, 1924, in Milton, Massachusetts

Party: Republican

Parents: Prescott Sheldon Bush, Dorothy Walker

First Lady: Barbara Pierce

Children: George, Robin, John, Neil, Marvin, Dorothy

Education: Yale University

Nickname: Poppy

Famous Firsts:

- The largest oil spill ever to take place in U.S. waters occurred when the *Exxon-Valdez* struck a reef near an Alaskan port. Nearly eleven million gallons of crude oil spilled into the ocean.
- Bush and Soviet leader Mikhail Gorbachev signed the first treaty to call for reduction in the existing long-range nuclear weapons (START I).
- He was the first future president to request, in writing, the resignation of a current president, Richard M. Nixon.

Achievements:

- Bush was a war hero who received the Distinguished Flying Cross for his heroism in World War II when his plane was shot down.
- Bush was an independently wealthy oilman in Texas before entering politics.
- From 1976–1977, Bush was the head of the Central Intelligence Agency (CIA).
- Bush sent troops to Somalia to help end the mass starvation there.
- Bush made significant strides with Russian relations. During his time in office, the Strategic Arms Reduction Treaties (START I and START II) were signed.

Interesting Facts:

- Bush was acting president for eight hours while President Ronald Reagan was in surgery for cancer.
- His father was a senator from Connecticut for several years.
- Barbara Bush's father was the publisher of *McCall's* and *Redbook* magazines.
- Bush was captain of the baseball team during his senior year at Yale.
- In college, Bush was elected to the Phi Beta Kappa honor society.
- As vice president to Ronald Reagan, Bush enjoyed a more active role than past vice presidents.
- Bush suffered from Graves' disease, a disorder of the thyroid gland that gave him an irregular heartbeat.

Presidential Quiz

Test your knowledge of the three 1980s presidents with this quiz. Read the words, events, and names in each row. Determine which president is most connected with them. Circle C for Carter, R for Reagan, and B for Bush.

1.   **C**   **R**   **B**   Points of Light Initiative, literacy

2.   **C**   **R**   **B**   Sandra Day O'Connor, Elizabeth Dole

3.   **C**   **R**   **B**   Iranian hostage crisis, Department of Energy created

4.   **C**   **R**   **B**   CHALLENGER, war on drugs

5.   **C**   **R**   **B**   Camp David peace talks, Three Mile Island accident

6.   **C**   **R**   **B**   Dan Quayle, "read my lips"

7.   **C**   **R**   **B**   assassination attempt, Star Wars

8.   **C**   **R**   **B**   human rights, gas shortages

9.   **C**   **R**   **B**   William Rehnquist, Antonin Scalia

10.   **C**   **R**   **B**   budget deficit, hostages freed

11.   **C**   **R**   **B**   boat people, Moral Majority

12.   **C**   **R**   **B**   *Exxon-Valdez*, Strategic Arms Reduction Treaties

13.   **C**   **R**   **B**   peanut-farming business, Habitat for Humanity

14.   **C**   **R**   **B**   Distinguished Flying Cross award, oilman

15.   **C**   **R**   **B**   Panama Canal Treaty, SALT II agreement

16.   **C**   **R**   **B**   Central Intelligence Agency (CIA), Somalian famine

17.   **C**   **R**   **B**   nuclear treaty, Iran-Contra

18.   **C**   **R**   **B**   Soviet Olympic boycott, Live Aid

19.   **C**   **R**   **B**   California Governor, president of Screen Actors Guild

20.   **C**   **R**   **B**   gave aid to Sandinistas, energy crisis

Assassination Attempt

On a quiet Monday in the nation's capital, just two months after taking office, President Ronald Reagan and several other officials exited the Hilton Hotel. At 2:30 P.M., just moments after they had stepped onto the sidewalk, six shots rang out while the president was waving to the assembled crowd. The date was March 30, 1981.

While bodyguards tried to shield Reagan and a Secret Service agent unhesitantly pushed the president into his waiting car, other agents wrestled the lone gunman to the ground. However, a number of individuals the gunman had struck were also lying on the ground, including Press Secretary James Brady, a police officer, and a Secret Service agent. As the nation would learn shortly, the seventy-year-old president had also been hit.

The wounded president was rushed to George Washington University Hospital where a bullet was discovered to be lodged in his left lung, close to his heart. Doctors said that had the bullet been an inch or two closer, the shot would certainly have been fatal. However, the doctors were able to remove the bullet, and Reagan went on to have an amazingly quick and complete recovery.

Unfortunately, all were not so lucky. While no one died at the hands of the gunman, James Brady was wounded in the head, and reports of his death were aired on the news off and on throughout the day. Finally, the nation learned that Brady had survived the wound but was permanently disabled; his recovery would be a long and arduous one.

Upon learning that the gunman had been captured, Reagan asked, "Does anybody know what that guy's beef was?" He and the nation were shocked to learn that the shooter had no political agenda. His name was John Hinckley, Jr., the son of a wealthy Texas oilman. Hinckley was a drifter with a history of psychological problems. His motive for the assassination attempt was apparently love. While watching a movie starring the actress Jodie Foster, Hinckley is said to have fallen in love with her. Apparently, an assassination attempt in the movie gave him his idea to kill the president as a means of showing his love to Foster. Hinckley was declared insane and sent to a mental hospital.

Reagan earned the nation's admiration when he returned to the White House in just two weeks. Reports of the president's bravery and humor abounded. Many people relayed the story of how Reagan, upon seeing his wife for the first time after the shooting, was said to have declared, "Honey, I forgot to duck." The nation became tremendously endeared to Reagan, and such public support likely became an aid to Reagan's ensuing success in the months that followed.

Yet mixed with the support for Reagan were scenes in the nation's consciousness of the wounded James Brady lying in a pool of his own blood on the sidewalk outside the Hilton. These images would also stay with legislators, who in the years to come gathered in support of certain anti-gun legislation created in Brady's name. However, the battle of gun control has continued to be a controversial topic throughout the remainder of the century.

Suggested Activities

Discussion: The assassination attempt on President Reagan, as well as the wounding of those around him, was shown repeatedly on national television throughout the day of the shooting. As a class, discuss the pros and cons of airing such acts of violence on television.

What Next? Learn about what has become of James Brady since the shooting. His name has been in the news on several occasions, particularly surrounding the legislation that he and his wife have supported.

Ladies in the House

The first ladies of the 1980s were all actively involved in various causes, and continued to be so when life in the White House had ended. Following is information regarding each of the three first ladies and the causes for which they have stridently worked.

Rosalynn Carter

Born Rosalynn Smith on August 18, 1927, Rosalynn Carter attended college for a short while, leaving to marry her high school sweetheart, Jimmy Carter, in 1946. The couple had four children, three sons and daughter Amy (who lived with them later in the White House).

Beginning in 1953, the Carters ran the family agriculture business, and then Rosalynn worked in support of her husband's political career. During his presidency, she often represented him at ceremonial occasions, and she attended Cabinet meetings and major briefings as well. She also served as the president's personal emissary to Latin American countries during her time in the White House.

Rosalynn Carter is remembered as one of the most socially active first ladies in history. Causes important to her included, among other things, the performing arts. She often invited classical artists to the White House to perform. Mrs. Carter also worked with programs to aid mental health, to support communities, and to benefit the elderly. From 1977 to 1978, she served as the Honorary Chairperson of the President's Commission on Mental Health. After leaving the White House, the Carters opened The Carter Center in Atlanta, Georgia, founded in 1982, for the purpose of promoting peace, democracy, and humanitarian causes. The couple have also been instrumental in supporting Habitat for Humanity, an organization that builds low-income housing for the impoverished and needy.

Nancy Reagan

Born Anne Francis Robbins in New York City, on July 6, 1923, Nancy Reagan was adopted by her stepfather, neurosurgeon Loyal Davis, when she was fourteen years old. She attended and graduated from Smith College, and then she went to Hollywood where she made eleven movies from 1949-1956. In 1952, she married Ronald Reagan. Reagan had two children by his first wife, and Nancy and Ronald had two more children.

Mrs. Reagan did not take the active role in her husband's presidency that Rosalynn Carter had done; however, she also worked diligently for causes important to her heart. These included the Foster Grandparents Program and the fight against drug and alcohol abuse in young people. The Foster Grandparents Program was begun in 1965. It engages seniors as mentors, tutors, and nurturers of children with special needs. It is a federally funded program through the Corps of Volunteer Service.

Mrs. Reagan is perhaps best known for her work against drug abuse. She is quoted as stating, "Say 'yes' to life, and when it comes to drugs and alcohol, just say 'no.'" "Just say no" became the slogan of her anti-drug campaign, and to this day it is a message taught to children throughout the United States and other nations as well. The message was meant to combat peer pressure and to help children take ownership of their own lives and health.

Ladies in the House *(cont.)*

Nancy Reagan *(cont.)*

Finally, in 1994, former President Reagan announced to the world his personal struggle with Alzheimer's disease. Due to their experiences, the Reagans, together with the National Alzheimer's Association, opened the Ronald and Nancy Reagan Research Institute to help find treatments for the disease and, hopefully, a cure.

Barbara Bush

Born in Rye, New York, on June 8, 1925, Barbara Pierce attended Smith College for two years and then left to marry George Bush. The two had six children, five of whom grew to adulthood. The sixth, Robin, died in 1953 of leukemia at the age of three.

Mrs. Bush was never quite as much in the spotlight as her two predecessors; however, she, too, was committed to some important causes. Among the fights closest to her heart were helping the homeless, fighting drug abuse, and combating illiteracy. In 1989, Barbara Bush launched the Barbara Bush Foundation for Family Literacy. Believing that illiteracy affects the quality of life of an individual, his or her ability to participate in society, and the future success and literacy of his or her children, Mrs. Bush began the foundation to develop and expand family literacy throughout the nation. She believes that increased literacy will decrease a variety of other ills plaguing the nation. Her foundation is committed to breaking the intergenerational cycle of illiteracy and to developing programs that will promote family literacy. To this end, various grants in high amounts are offered annually to groups promoting and increasing such literacy.

One additional cause important to both the Bushes is that of finding a cure for leukemia, the disease that took the life of their young daughter. Mrs. Bush often visits cancer patients and volunteers her time in fundraising efforts. She also volunteers in a number of homeless shelters and soup kitchens. Her books, *C. Fred's Story: A Dog's Life* (1984) and *Millie's Book: As Dictated to Barbara Bush* (1990), were published to generate funds to support Bush's charitable interests.

Suggested Activities

Causes: Research to find out more about one of the important causes championed by the first ladies of the eighties. Find out how you can become involved as a class, in groups, or individually. Share your work with the class. Discuss how one individual can make a difference.

Celebrity and Publicity: Discuss the role that celebrity has in promoting causes and whether or not individuals should take advantage of their celebrity to put forward their ideas.

Election Facts and Figures

	Election of 1980	Election of 1984	Election of 1988
Democrats	President Jimmy Carter and Vice President Walter F. Mondale ran once more.	Former Vice President Walter Mondale took as his running mate Representative Geraldine A. Ferraro of New York, the first woman ever nominated to the presidential ticket of a major party.	Governor Michael S. Dukakis of Massachusetts was nominated with long-time Senator Lloyd Bentsen of Texas as his running mate.
Republicans	Ronald Wilson Reagan, former actor and California governor, ran with running mate George Bush.	President Reagan and Vice President Bush were easily nominated again by their party.	Vice President George Herbert Walker Bush was nominated for the candidacy. Senator Dan Quayle of Indiana was nominated as his running mate.
Other	Representative John Anderson of Illinois broke with the Republican Party to run as an Independent.	No other major candidates surfaced during this election.	No other major candidates surfaced during this election.
Issues	The primary issues were inflation, unemployment, and taxes. Seriously dampening Carter's chances was the hostage situation in Iran. Reagan urged his "supply-side theory of economics," an emphasis on tax reduction to stimulate business activity.	Economic growth, US–Soviet relations, and inflation were the primary issues.	Bush attacked Dukakis' lack of experience in foreign affairs and track record of leniency in some criminal cases. Dukakis questioned Bush's avowed lack of knowledge in the Iran-Contra affair, and he pointed out the many social service programs that had been cut or terminated under the Reagan-Bush administration.
Winner	Prior to the election, analysts thought the race would be close. However, Reagan took 489 electoral votes to Carter's 49. The popular vote was about 44 million to 35 million. An Independent candidate, John Anderson of Illinois, earned about 5.5 million popular votes. At age 69, Reagan became the oldest president elected.	In a sweeping landslide, Reagan took 525 electoral votes to Mondale's 13. The popular vote was about 54.5 million for Reagan and 37.5 million for Mondale.	Bush won the election with 436 electoral votes to Dukakis' 111. The popular vote was closer with approximately 49 million going to the Republicans and 42 million to the Democrats. Interestingly, vice-presidential nominee Bentsen earned one electoral vote of his own.

More About the Elections

Here are some ways to use the Election Facts and Figures on page 29. Select those activities and projects which best suit your classroom needs.

1. Prepare a classroom chart with five different sections, each marked with a vice-presidential candidate's name from the 1980s (from the major party tickets). Pair the students. Allow each pair to select a candidate's name, or randomly assign them. Instruct the pairs to find out more about the men and woman nominated for vice president: where they were born, their childhoods and schooling, their political backgrounds, what became of them after the election or after office, and so forth. Compile all the information gathered onto your prepared chart.

2. President Reagan won by a wide margin in both of his elections. Research as a class to determine the reasons Reagan won so handily.

3. Percentages of electoral votes do not always seem to reflect the percentages of popular votes. Have the students study the electoral system to determine how it works. They can then take sides in a debate over this system of electing a president.

4. Many people say that Presidents Carter and Reagan were elected because of the popular desire for change from all that had come before. Research to find out the truth of this statement and why the nation would desire a change.

5. The hostages held in Iran were probably instrumental in incumbent President Carter's loss of the 1980 election. Learn about the hostage situation, and discuss the relevancy of their release on Reagan's inaugural day.

6. The 1980s were a strongly Republican time. What effect did this have on the nation? Learn about the conservative changes throughout the nation in the eighties and what happened into the nineties.

7. Rev. Jesse Jackson was an important part of the election of 1984. Learn about the effect his bid for the presidency had on the eventual outcome of the election.

8. Geraldine Ferraro became the first woman to run for vice president on a major party ticket. Learn about Ferraro's political perspectives and values. Then, as a class, discuss how her election with presidential hopeful Walter Mondale might have affected the nation.

9. Extend the information provided on page 29 with other facts and figures. For example, find out how many popular votes the candidates garnered in their respective elections. Make a chart comparing the figures. See page 31 for some math problems that use these figures.

10. Ronald Reagan became the oldest elected president in 1980. Discuss as a class the effects that age has, if any, on a high-level leadership position. Remind students that the minimum age for the presidency is thirty-five.

Election Math

In the chart below, you will find the number of electoral votes and popular votes for each presidential election of the eighties (using statistics for the major party tickets only). Use this chart to answer the questions that follow. Show your work.

Year	Candidate	Electoral Vote	Popular Vote
1980	Carter	49	35,484,000
	Reagan	489	43,904,000
1984	Mondale	13	37,577,000
	Reagan	525	54,455,000
1988	Dukakis	111	41,805,374
	Bush	436	48,881,278

1. How many more electoral votes were there in 1988 than in 1984?

2. How many popular votes were there altogether in 1980?

3. How many total electoral votes in all three elections?

4. Using the figure from problem #3, what is the average number of electoral votes per election?

5. Using the answer from problem #4, which actual number of electoral votes (total from one election) comes closest to the average number?

6. What is the combined number of popular votes that Reagan received in his two elections?

7. What percentage of popular votes did Carter receive in 1980? (Round the answer.)

8. What percentage of electoral votes did Carter receive in 1980? (Round the answer.)

Chernobyl and the *Exxon-Valdez*

In each decade there are sure to be a variety of natural disasters, such as earthquakes and hurricanes, that strike areas around the world. These disasters often claim many lives and destroy millions of dollars in property. In the eighties, two disasters with far–reaching consequences were caused not by forces of nature but by human error.

The worst nuclear accident ever known occurred on April 26, 1986, near Kiev, Ukraine, which was at the time part of the Soviet Union. One of four reactors at the Chernobyl nuclear power plant went out of control. Due to improper supervision, the water cooling system turned off. This led to an uncontrolled reaction which caused a steam explosion. As a result, the roof was blown off the building, releasing massive amounts of radioactive material into the atmosphere. The radiation easily spread from the eastern Soviet Union to northern and central Europe, causing much concern throughout the area and, in fact, the world. Radiation counts jumped to 1,000 times their norm. Farm crops and grazing lands were contaminated as far away as Poland, Scotland, and Great Britain.

According to the Soviets, thirty-one people died immediately of burns and exposure to radiation, and more than 300 were injured seriously. However, these numbers are debated elsewhere, and many people believe that they are, in reality, much higher. Medical experts generally believe that there will prove to be an increase in cancer experienced by those closest to the accident. More than 100,000 Soviet citizens were evacuated from the areas surrounding the reactor site.

Three years after the Chernobyl accident, the world's attention shifted to Prince William Sound in southeastern Alaska. The Exxon Corporation, the largest petroleum company in the world, was transporting oil from the Trans-Alaska Pipeline on March 24, 1989. Its tanker, the *Exxon-Valdez*, ran aground and began leaking oil. The leakage continued for two days, spilling nearly eleven million gallons (42 million liters) of crude oil into the water. This was the largest oil spill in North American history. Thousands of marine animals and birds were killed, and 1,100 miles (1,770 km) of Alaska's shoreline were contaminated. Cleanup of the spill cost Exxon approximately two billion dollars. Criminal charges were filed against the company by the United States government in 1990; a plea bargain was accepted in 1991. Exxon agreed to pay $1,025,000,000 in penalties and the company pleaded guilty to four misdemeanor charges.

Suggested Activities

Discussion: Discuss the following: Is nuclear power worth the risk to life and the environment?

Science: Learn about nuclear power and how it is manufactured. Also learn about the uses of crude oil.

Environment: What was involved in the cleanup of Prince Edward Sound? What about Chernobyl? Read to find the continuing costs to the environment since the time of both accidents, as well as what people are doing (and have done) to better the situations.

Mount Saint Helens

When Mount Saint Helens erupted on May 18, 1980, the blast was about 500 times more powerful than an atomic bomb and was heard 135 miles (217 kilometers) away.

The peak is located 95 miles (153 kilometers) south of Seattle, Washington, in the Cascade Mountains. When it erupted, 57 people died, and the combination of heat, hot mud, ash, rock, and residual fires caused the deaths of countless birds and animals as well as the destruction of a hundred thousand acres of forest. More than 1,000 feet (300 meters) was blown from the top of the mountain, resulting in hundreds of millions of dollars in damages.

The eruption of Mount Saint Helens was the first to take place in the contiguous United States since 1917, when California's Lassen Peak erupted. Mount Saint Helens itself had been inactive from 1857 until that fateful day in 1980.

When the mountain erupted, the heat caused a great deal of snow to melt, and flooding and mud slides added to the countless other tragedies of the volcanic activity. The most pervasive effect was the layer of ash that spread over an extensive area, destroying crops and polluting the air. People as far away as Oregon and Idaho were affected. Many people wore surgical masks when they were outdoors to filter the ash and protect their lungs. Many car engines and a variety of machines were ruined by the ash as well.

In a few months the ash had settled, and solidified lava capped the mountain. Over the next six years, many minor eruptions occurred, but they did not do extensive damage. Mount Saint Helens is expected to continue to erupt during the coming years.

Suggested Activities

Geology: Learn about the three types of volcanoes: cinder cones, shield volcanoes, and composite volcanoes. What are their similarities and differences? Create charts and drawings to show your findings.

Claims to Fame: A number of volcanoes have become famous over the years. Identify as many of the following as possible, telling about their famous eruptions and what type of volcano each is: Aconcagua, Cotopaxi, El Chichón, Krakatau, Lassen Peak, Mauna Loa, Mont Pelée, Mount Etna, Mount Pinatubo, Mount Tambora, Nevado del Ruiz, Paricutin, Stromboli, Surtsey, Thira (formerly Santorin), and Vesuvius.

San Francisco Revisited

Very few were left who remembered the terrible San Francisco earthquake of 1906 and its consequences, but on October 17, 1989, a whole new generation experienced a similar natural disaster firsthand. A magnitude 7.1 earthquake struck the entire Bay Area just moments before the third game of the 1989 World Series was to take place at Candlestick Park. Thirty-seven minutes later, a 5.2 aftershock hit. The results were dramatic, terrifying, and tragic.

Called the Loma Prieta Earthquake, the tremor struck at precisely 5:04:21 P.M., Pacific Daylight Time. The earthquake's epicenter was in a remote section of the Santa Cruz Mountains, nearly sixty miles southeast of San Francisco. Motion recorders felt the tremor at various intervals: 5:04:21 at the epicenter, 5:04:31 at Candlestick Park, 5:04:37 at San Francisco's Presidio, and twenty-two seconds later in Sacramento, one hundred miles away.

The effects of the earthquake to lives and property were devastating. Relatively few people (11) died as a direct result of the quake, but more than 3,700 people were injured, over 12,000 were left homeless, and damage to property exceeded ten billion dollars. Thirty-six fires were reported to the San Francisco Fire Department from October 17 at the time of the earthquake to October 19; all but two of these were directly attributed to the quake and its aftershocks. Most of San Francisco also lost its electricity when the earthquake hit, causing the entire city to go dark for the first time since the 1906 quake. Buildings collapsed or were condemned, and an entire section of the San Francisco-Oakland Bay Bridge buckled. A fire broke out at the 911 telephone equipment room, causing emergency telephone service to become sporadic. The tremor also triggered a tsunami in Monterey Bay and an undersea landslide, causing the sea level at Santa Cruz to drop three feet. Freeway sections were rocked so vigorously that they cracked in various places and several columns fractured.

1906 was also revisited in scenes of "bucket brigades" created by citizens in order to help fire fighters who were without water due to broken water mains. Within moments of the devastation, people everywhere were rallying together to help one another. However, some people turned to crime and looting, to which the District Attorney, Arlo Smith, quickly responded, "Anyone engaged in that kind of conduct can expect maximum sentences." One such petty thief, DeSoto Barker, was shot and killed by a frustrated motorist when the former stole traffic flares.

Just as it had done in 1906, San Francisco rallied and began to rebuild. The process was sometimes slow, but the effects of the earthquake were eventually eradicated, and the city thrived once more.

Suggested Activities

Compare: Make a chart comparing the geology and effects of the 1906 and 1989 San Francisco earthquakes.

Science: Conduct experiments that demonstrate how earthquakes operate and what their effects can be.

Geology: Study the dynamics of earthquakes and why they happen.

Elsewhere: Learn about other sites of tragic earthquakes throughout history. Why do earthquakes of less magnitude than the San Francisco quake sometimes have more devastating results?

AIDS

First identified by doctors in 1980 and 1981, Acquired Immune Deficiency Syndrome (AIDS) became a major issue of the eighties. Since 1981, AIDS has been found in more than 150 countries around the world. The World Health Organization estimates that there may be more than twenty million HIV and AIDS cases by the turn of the century.

In the early eighties, doctors began to see an increase in rare forms of cancer, pneumonia, and serious infections among previously healthy young men. Until then, these infections and diseases occurred mainly in transplant patients. The doctors soon found evidence that the syndrome spread through direct blood contact or an exchange of bodily fluids. In 1983 and 1984, scientists in France and the United States isolated a retrovirus from AIDS patients and identified it as the cause of AIDS. They named the virus Human Immunodeficiency Virus, or HIV. French researchers then isolated another virus, HIV-2, which occurs mainly in Africa.

HIV attaches itself to certain white blood cells that are essential in the normal functioning of the immune system. The virus then inserts its genes into these cells, where it replicates itself and progressively destroys the immune system. HIV can be present in a person for two to twelve years before any symptoms occur and can be transmitted to another person even if there are no symptoms. Scientists do not know exactly how or where HIV infections began. Similar viruses exist in some African monkeys and other animal populations, but these viruses do not affect humans. Researchers have shown that people died of AIDS as early as the sixties and seventies.

To date, there is no known cure for or vaccine against HIV infection. Education and research have been the focus of the battle against AIDS since the early eighties. In 1987, a drug known as AZT became the first antiviral drug approved in the United States for HIV and AIDS infection. New drug therapies focus on preventing replication of HIV within the cells of infected people. Widespread educational campaigns teach people preventive measures and encourage testing for the virus.

Throughout the eighties, AIDS patients and their families suffered from ostracism and violence caused by the mistaken belief that AIDS could be "caught" by touching an infected person or sitting near him or her. In 1987, a family in Florida received bomb threats when their three sons, all infected with AIDS through blood transfusions, tried to attend the local school. Others, like teenage victim Ryan White, led a campaign of education to heighten public awareness and to spread accurate information about AIDS.

In the nineties, research and public education continued, as did the controversy about the ways in which HIV is spread and the preventive measures sometimes suggested. Meanwhile, scientists remain hopeful for a cure.

Suggested Activities

Science: Learn more about HIV and AIDS, focusing on the physiology of retroviruses.

Status Report: Research to learn the latest developments in the battle against this epidemic.

Magic Johnson: One of the most important events in the history of this disease occurred in 1991 when basketball superstar Magic Johnson, a young, strong, popular athlete, announced that he had tested positive for HIV. How, if at all, did this announcement affect the public's perception of HIV and AIDS. When, after time off, Johnson decided to return to the sport he had helped revolutionize, how did the athletic community react? With practical concern? irrational fear? acceptance?

Environmentalism

Throughout the decade, environmentalism was an issue at the forefront of political debate, social action, and public awareness. Concerns first expressed in the sixties and seventies gained new audiences. People became interested in the quality of air and water, the survival of the rain forest, the depletion of the ozone layer, and other issues. Curbing pollution, recycling, and stopping waste were prominent themes.

Suggested Activity

Environmental Bingo: Complete three in a row on the bingo card below, or make your own card and fill it in. In order to mark a space, the task must be completed.

Environmental Bingo		
Find a water leak at home, school, or in a local business. Report it.	Snip each section of a six-pack ring before you discard it.	Clean out your closet or cupboard and, with your parent's permission, donate things you do not want to a needy organization.
Next time you find a bug in your home or classroom, do not kill it. Help it get back outside safely.	Create your own ecology project such as a newsletter, fund-raising event, play, or letter-writing campaign to help others become environmentally aware.	Use a recycling box at home for paper, taking it to a recycling center when the box is full.
Construct an art project from recycled material.	Turn off the water while you brush your teeth, turning it on only for rinsing.	For a week, use only cloth towels and napkins.

Homelessness

Homelessness is a condition that has existed throughout time, but the 1980s saw not only an increase in the numbers of homeless but also a shift in the demographics and a recognition of the condition as a significant social problem. By 1985, estimates for the number of homeless people in the nation ranged from 300,000 to several million; yet, there were fewer than 100,000 beds available in public shelters for these displaced individuals. The problem in America had become worse than at any time since the Great Depression.

Traditionally, people saw the homeless population as older, white, alcoholic men—those who populated the "skid rows" of the forties and fifties. By the 1980s, most of the homeless were non-white, and while adult men still comprised the highest percentage of the homeless population, a quickly growing number of women and children were on the streets. Researchers say the reasons for the increases in female and youth homelessness included spousal abuse (causing some women and their children to flee from abusive husbands and fathers) and the rise in teenage runaways.

Causes for homelessness vary, but researchers conclude that most of the homeless are very poor and estranged from their families and other systems of support. About one-third of the adult homeless are thought to be mentally ill and another half addicted to drugs and alcohol. Approximately one-third of homeless men are believed to be war veterans.

Why the rates of homelessness increased so dramatically in the eighties is not simple to ascertain; however, the total rate of poverty did increase during this time. Most effected were inner cities, where many of the homeless dwelled. In these areas, there was a significant drop in the availability of low-income housing. Also during the 1980s, the government shut down a number of hospitals and institutions where the mentally ill had lived. Many of these people found their way to the streets. Finally, the rate of violence against women increased, and often those women had no place to go but to the streets.

In addition to those who were actually homeless, there became a growing number of individuals (about twenty million) who were said to be "marginally housed." Those people paid seventy percent or better of their income toward housing. If economic challenges were to have struck them, it was conceivable that they would be instantly without a home. There were also many more individuals who had no home of their own but who had been taken in by their families in the hopes that they could find employment enough to support themselves. These were called the "hidden homeless."

In 1986, a group of activists went on a hunger strike in Washington, D.C., hoping to raise funds for homeless shelters. Elsewhere, groups of homeless individuals conducted similar protests. However, most help for the homeless does not come from the government but from private institutions, such as churches and charitable organizations, and from caring individuals. The primary federal program for the homeless was created in 1987. The Stewart B. McKinney Homeless Assistance Act established a network of health clinics for the homeless, as well as adult education programs, emergency homelessness prevention funds, and transitional housing programs.

Suggested Activity

Solution: As a class, brainstorm solutions for the homeless crisis. Is the problem one that belongs to the government, to the private sector, or to both?

Live Aid

In the early eighties, famine struck the nation of Ethiopia, killing countless people through starvation and malnutrition. People around the world gave their sympathy, but not everyone rallied to help the people's plight. One who did was Irish rock star Bob Geldof. Geldof was perhaps most noted for his performance in the rock film *The Wall* (based on the album by the classic group Pink Floyd.)

Bob Geldof

Geldof became aware of the famine through the news media, just as most other people did. However, he felt driven to make a difference.

In 1984, Bob Geldof organized the recording of a collaborative song for release during the Christmas season. It was entitled "Do They Know It's Christmas?" The song tells of the trouble in Africa, asking the people of the world to look outside of their own small spheres to see the starving people in Ethiopia for whom Christmas and other joys would mean nothing when compared to their life-threatening circumstances. Music superstars from several nations joined together in collaboration on the record, and it became one of the most successful records of the year.

However, this success was not enough for Geldof. He took the momentum of the song and organized two of the largest rock concerts ever and called them Live Aid. On July 7, 1985, the two concerts were broadcast around the world, and statistics show that one-third of the world's population watched at least a portion of the concerts live. One concert took place in Philadelphia's JFK Stadium and the other in London's Wembley Stadium. Performers for the concerts included such music stars as The Who, Madonna, Paul McCartney, U2, Led Zeppelin, Bob Dylan, and Dire Straits. Throughout the shows, the performers asked listeners to donate money for Ethiopian famine relief. In all, approximately $53 million was raised.

Live Aid became a catalyst for other such efforts, including Farm Aid which continued to be held annually well into the nineties to help American farmers keep their farms.

Suggested Activities

Listening: Close your eyes and listen to a recording of "Do They Know It's Christmas?" Afterwards, without talking, write your responses to the song.

Making a Difference: As a class, brainstorm for ways in which you might make a difference in relieving world hunger. Together, choose one of your ideas to do. Be sure to follow through with the idea to completion. It will benefit the students tremendously to see how they can make a difference.

"First Ladies"

Many women came to political prominence in the eighties. Three noteworthy women are Sandra Day O'Connor, Geraldine Ferraro, and Wilma Mankiller.

Sandra Day O'Connor was born in 1930 in El Paso, Texas, and she received a Stanford University law degree in 1952. In 1965, she became attorney general for Arizona, and, in 1969, was appointed to complete a term in the state senate. She was elected to the Arizona senate in the following year and again in 1972, and she was senate majority leader in 1973. O'Connor became a judge of a county trial court in 1974, and, in 1979, she was appointed by the Arizona governor to the state court of appeals, the second highest court in the state.

O'Connor came to national prominence when United States Supreme Court Justice Potter Stewart retired in 1981. President Ronald Reagan, in one of the earliest acts of his presidency, named her to fill the vacancy. She accepted and was approved by Congress in a vote of 99–0 (with one abstention).

Sandra Day O'Conner

Associate Justice O'Connor's record of conservative perspectives as a judge made her an ideal candidate for the conservative president's appointment. However, the thing that drew most public attention to her was the fact that she was the first woman ever to be named to the United States Supreme Court. Many women at the time hoped that she would be an active proponent for women's rights; however, her activities have not indicated as such.

Geraldine Ferraro

Geraldine Ferraro also had a strong political career when she gained national attention for her role in national politics. She became the first woman to be nominated for vice president on a major party ticket. In the 1984 election, she was the running mate of Democratic presidential nominee and former Vice President Walter Mondale.

Ferraro, the daughter of Italian immigrants, was a lawyer and former assistant district attorney in Queens County, New York. She first won election to the United States House of Representatives in 1978. She continued in that office until 1984, when she received the Democratic vice-presidential nomination. She was chosen by the party not only for her political abilities but also for the express purpose of breaking traditions and political obstructions. The hope was to defeat popular President Reagan. A Mondale aide is quoted as saying, "She's a woman, she's ethnic, she's Catholic . . . we have broken the barrier."

"First Ladies" *(cont.)*

Although the Mondale-Ferraro ticket made a respectable showing in the months prior to the election, they lost the final election in one of the most drastic landslides in history, with Mondale-Ferraro taking only thirteen electoral votes. However, regardless of the major loss, the two will always be remembered for breaking new political ground.

Wilma Pearl Mankiller was born into poverty in the hills of Oklahoma in 1945. While attending college, she met a group of Native-American activists; Mankiller then realized that her mission was to serve her people. In 1985, she became the first woman to serve as the principal chief of the age-old Cherokee Nation. Her activities in that position have brought the Nation long overdue recognition in the United States and greater political weight than ever before.

Willma Mankiller

The history of the Cherokee people takes many turns, but many people remember the Cherokee in connection with the tragic Trail of Tears, the time in 1838 when 13,000 Cherokee were forcibly evacuated from their land in the southeast woodlands to Indian Territory, 1,000 miles (1,610 kilometers) away. The people were allowed to take nothing with them, and they were made to travel by foot. It is estimated that 4,000 died during the journey. Approximately 300 people hid in the Great Smoky Mountains of their homeland. Since that time, members of the Nation have been trying to rebuild it. Mankiller has made great leaps in doing just that.

Wilma Mankiller has worked diligently to preserve the history, traditions, and customs of the Cherokee Nation, as well as to carve the people a strong and important place in the United States. Under her leadership, the people have regained much of the tradition and pride that was lost to them over the years.

For her efforts, Wilma Mankiller was inducted into the Oklahoma Women's Hall of Fame in 1986. In 1993, she was named as one of the United States' outstanding women. Mankiller announced in 1995 that she would not seek re-election.

Suggested Activities

Politics: Learn more about the political views of Sandra Day O'Connor, Geraldine Ferraro, and Wilma Mankiller. In your opinion, would any of the women make a good candidate for the United States presidency?

Madam President: Some women have run for president, but not on a major party ticket. Look up one such woman, and research her political career.

Read: Wilma Mankiller's autobiography is called *Mankiller: A Chief and Her People* (St. Martin's Press, 1993). It is an excellent resource, telling not only about her life but about the history of the Cherokee Nation.

Discussion: Hold a class discussion on the topic of leadership and the sexes. Discuss if and how a person's sex affects his or her ability to lead.

Supreme Court: Learn about the Supreme Court of the United States and how it operates. Pay close attention to the decisions made since O'Connor's appointment.

Music Television (MTV)

The first music videos were used mainly to promote new groups and new songs. In the late 1970s, European record companies began showing well-produced music videos in nightclubs and on television. The result was increased sales. This persuaded American record producers to attempt something similar. In 1981, Warner Amex Satellite Entertainment Company (WASEC) launched Music Television (MTV) as a 24-hour music video channel.

It was patterned after existing radio formats, with an announcer called a VJ (video jockey) to present the segments and give other vital information in much the same way a disc jockey (DJ) does on the radio. Each rock music video would feature a three- to four-minute performance by the recording artist.

MTV began its broadcast with a video entitled "Video Killed the Radio Star"—and, indeed, video did transform the entire music industry. MTV brought rock videos into the mainstream and made the visual just as important as the audio for almost all pop music to come. In fact, some would argue that the visual became even more important. Music videos have become an art form, constantly seeking to achieve new video styles through the use of special effects. These styles have had an influence on television shows, commercials, and feature films. It is commonly asserted that some major rock stars of the eighties, like Madonna and Michael Jackson, skyrocketed to success because of their video presence.

The initial cost for MTV was twenty million dollars. In the first eighteen months, the channel had earned seven million dollars in ad revenues and, by mid-1983, it had 125 advertisers. Ad revenues reached a million a week by 1984, with an audience of approximately twenty million made up primarily of 12 to 34 year olds.

MTV developed exclusive rights to new videos with four record companies by mid-1984. At that time, it branched out into a second channel, VH-1, intending to reach an older audience by focusing on other forms of pop music, like soft rock. Competing video shows turned up on most major networks, but none reached the success of MTV.

By the end of the eighties, MTV had changed its format considerably, introducing a variety of regular programs, such as news and game shows, in addition to music videos. It also included a variety of music styles, focusing on rap and other forms that became popular over the years. Sometimes controversial for the sex and violence displayed in some rock videos, MTV has nonetheless grown into a powerhouse in the cable industry, as well as in the music industry.

Suggested Activities

View and Discuss: At your own discretion, view some music videos. Choose carefully and be sure to get the approval of your school administrators and students' parents. There are videos that are acceptable and are, in fact, worthy of discussion in social, as well as artistic terms.

Research: Study to find out the specific effects that MTV has had on the cable television and music industries. The effects, particularly on music, have been enormous.

Video Games

Video games are electronic games that are played on a display monitor while the player manipulates a button, mouse, joystick, and/or trackball. As any child of the eighties can tell you, video games were big business from the outset.

The business of video games began in the United States in the early seventies with a simple, tennis-type game called "Pong" that was attached to television sets for play. Other games followed, with video arcades sprouting up by the late seventies and early eighties. The 1980s saw rapid growth in the industry, but the industry itself nearly collapsed in the mid-eighties due to financial over-extension by such leading corporations as Atari. At this time, Japanese businesses took to the forefront, particularly the Nintendo Corporation, and "Donkey Kong" and "Super Mario Brothers" became the decade's latest crazes.

Former adolescent and teen hangouts were taken over by the growing video game industry. Arcades were placed in nearly every mall, and children of all ages could be seen crowding around "Ms. Pac-Man" while the pinball machines of times past lay virtually dormant. Of course, while the market grew, so did the variety and technology available, so much so that by the early 1990s enhanced graphics (like those seen at the arcades) were available for home entertainment systems.

Today the Japanese continue to dominate the market with such companies as Sega, Sony, and Nintendo. Millions of children across the nation own home video game systems, CD-ROM games to be used on their computers, and miniature handheld versions of the computerized games.

Games generally fall within three categories: learning, adventure, and sports. Sports games topped the market by the late eighties due to the big-name athletes and professional teams who lend their names to the products. Top sellers to this day are often those attached to a famous athlete's name. The most popular games are those with realistic sounds, fast-moving visual effects, and colorful graphics.

Along with the success of video games has come a number of criticisms, particularly from parents who think their children spend too much time and money on the games and that there is little value in them other than pure entertainment. Video games have also come under fire repeatedly for violent content, and science has found that the flashes of light from video games can trigger seizures in individuals with certain types of epilepsy. Supporters of the games insist that there is real educational value to many of them and that they teach problem-solving techniques, eye-hand coordination, and familiarity with computers. Nursing homes have also been known to use video games for both rehabilitation therapy and for entertainment.

Due to the backlash over violent content, Nintendo and Sega spearheaded a movement in 1993 to establish an industry-wide ratings system. Today the consumer can find ratings on the packaging of most video games for sale or rent.

Suggested Activities

Video Technology: Learn about the other video technology of the 1980s, particularly in the area of video recording with VCRs, both VHS and Beta.

Changing Times: Discuss the effect that video has had on families, societies, and culture. How are these changes for the best? Are there any ways in which they have created problems for society?

Olympic Stars

The Olympic Games in the eighties were marked by controversy and triumph.

At the 1980 Winter Olympics in Lake Placid, New York, the impossible—or so many people thought—happened: the United States hockey team won the gold medal. Comprised of twenty college students, the U.S. team first defeated the team from the Soviet Union, a group of players that most experts believed to be the greatest in the world. Not only did they beat the Soviets, they went on to beat the team from Finland to become the gold medal winners. No U.S. hockey team had ever won the gold. In fact, the U.S. team was usually not even considered a contender. These were mere amateurs against the best professionals. It was an awesome victory.

Not to be outdone, Eric Heiden, a twenty-one-year-old speed skater, took home gold medals in all of the men's speed skating events. He became the first athlete to win five gold medals in one Winter Olympics.

The Summer Olympics of the same year were to be held in Moscow, but the events were overshadowed by a conflict in Afghanistan. In response to the Soviet invasion of Afghanistan, President Jimmy Carter imposed an embargo against the U.S.S.R. The Soviets refused to remove their troops, and Carter pressured the U.S. Olympic Committee to boycott the Games. Athletes from the United States and more than forty other nations did not participate. The Games were dominated by the Soviets and its allies.

The Soviets took their turn and boycotted the 1984 Summer Olympics in Los Angeles, California. The reason they gave was that the Games in L.A. were too commercial and that security would be too weak to protect their athletes. The Soviet-bloc nations joined in the boycott. Despite the absence of the Soviets and about six other nations, the Games were competitive and exciting. Track sensation Carl Lewis and gymnast Mary Lou Retton were the stars of the Games. Lewis took four gold medals, and Retton became the first American to win the gold in the women's all-around gymnastics category. She also took home four other gold medals.

No one boycotted the Summer Olympics of 1988 in Seoul, South Korea, and politics had almost no part in them. However, they were marred to some extent by the presence of illegal drugs. Track star Ben Johnson of Canada amazed the world with his record 100-meter dash, but six days later the gold medal was taken from him because of his use of anabolic steroids, drugs that increase physical stamina and performance. Ten other athletes were also disqualified during the Games for use of steroids.

Two other athletes came to international attention during the 1988 Summer Games, track stars Florence Griffith-Joyner and Jackie Joyner-Kersee.

Suggested Activity

Research: Learn more about any of the athletes named above and what has become of them since the time of the Olympics.

Bonnie the Blur

Bonnie was born the youngest of six children to Charles and Eleanor Blair of Cornwall, New York. The Blairs were a family of speed skaters, so much so that when Bonnie was being born, her father was training her older siblings on the ice. The ice rink announcer let everyone know, including Charles, that his new daughter had been born. The date was March 18, 1964.

It was inevitable that Bonnie would skate. Soon after she began walking, her family found the smallest pair of skates they could. Still too large, she wore her shoes inside the skates to make them fit. She was just two years old, but she immediately took to the ice.

The family moved to Champaign, Illinois, where winter skating was exceptional and indoor rinks were numerous. Young Bonnie was regularly on the ice, and at the age of four she skated in her first race. By age seven she was racing in the state championships. In 1981, at age seventeen, she took her first national title in Olympic-style racing. Although she was short for a speed skater (just 5' 4$\frac{1}{2}$"), she had tremendous leg and back strength and had developed a strong starting technique. It was at this time that Charles Blair began to dream of his daughter winning an Olympic gold. Shortly thereafter, Bonnie also caught gold fever, and Charles' dream became hers. Training for the 1984 Olympics began.

For Blair, getting the necessary funds to go to the 1984 Winter Olympics in Sarajevo, Yugoslavia, proved to be a challenge. The Champaign police force came to her rescue. They held raffles, bake sales, garage sales, candy sales, and even sold bumper stickers that read "Favorite Speeder." They raised $10,000 for the skater. She and a few members of her family traveled to Sarajevo. Bonnie did not win a medal in Sarajevo, but it was a valuable experience. Meanwhile, in 1983, 1984, and 1986, she did became the U.S. indoor speedskating champion, earning the nickname "Bonnie the Blur," and in 1986, she held the North American indoor title. She was ready for the 1988 Olympics in Calgary, Canada.

This time, the entire Blair family went along to watch the littlest sister compete, and Bonnie made them proud. She set a world record of 39.1 seconds in the 500-meter race, taking home the gold medal.

In 1989, Blair won the world all-over sprint title, and she placed second in 1990 and third in 1991. On Christmas Day, 1989, Charles Blair died of lung cancer, but Bonnie continued her training. She was accepted for the 1992 Olympics in Albertville, France, and there she became the first woman in Olympic history to win consecutive gold medals in the 500-meter race. She also took the gold in the 1,000 meter race. In 1993, she won the prestigious Sullivan Award, one of the highest honors for an amateur athlete. She followed this in 1994 with two more golds in the 500- and 1000-meter races at the Olympic Games in Lillehammer, Norway. She won the 1000 by just two hundredths of a second. She topped it all when one month later she broke the thirty-nine second barrier that had been her challenge, skating the 500 in 38.99 seconds. In 1995, she beat that record with a time of 38.69.

Bonnie Blair holds the record for the most Olympic gold medals won by an American woman.

Suggested Activity

Skating: Learn about the dynamics of speed skating as compared to figure skating. If possible, go skating as a class. Skate 500 meters to see how closely you come to Bonnie Blair's time!

Flo Jo

She is remembered for the nails and the one-legged running suits. Most of all, though she is remembered for the speed. Florence Griffith-Joyner was born on December 21, 1959. In 1964, the Griffiths moved to a housing project in Watts, an impoverished section of Los Angeles. However, the young girl did not feel poor. Of her childhood, she said, "We were rich as a family."

Griffith-Joyner first began running in the Mojave Desert while visiting her father who lived there. She tried to chase the jackrabbits living in the fields. Her mother noticed her athletic skills and encouraged her talents. Griffith-Joyner entered her first competition at the age of seven and won.

After graduating high school, she went on to attend Cal State Northridge. Also attending was her fiercest competitor to date, Valerie Brisco. Griffith-Joyner began work on a business degree while competing with the track team. However, after her freshman year, she felt she needed to drop out to earn money for the rest of her education. The young track coach, Bob Kersee, felt differently and helped her to acquire the financial aid she needed.

When Kersee was recruited to the University of California at Los Angeles (UCLA), Griffith-Joyner followed him there, believing that he was the best coach for her. While attending UCLA, her track abilities soared, and she was invited to compete in the 1980 Olympic trials. She came within inches of making the team—Brisco took the spot instead. Griffith-Joyner went instead to the NCAA championship in 1982, winning the 200-meter run. It was then, at UCLA, that Griffith-Joyner began to show her individual style on the track. She sported long, brightly painted fingernails. By the time she made the Olympic team in 1984, her trademark running clothes had earned her the nickname "Fluorescent Flo."

At the 1984 Olympics, Griffith-Joyner won the silver medal in the 200-meter dash. Her old rival, Valerie Brisco, took the gold. Besides the disappointment of losing to her rival, the silver award was also tarnished by the fact that many competitors were not at these Olympic Games, which were being boycotted by several nations. Also adding to the disappointment was the fact that Joyner missed running on the relay team, which won a gold medal, because she refused to cut her nails.

After these Olympics, Griffith-Joyner gave up running. Shortly thereafter, she began dating Olympic gold medalist Al Joyner, whose sister Jackie was also part of Florence's UCLA team. (Jackie married Coach Kersee.) With such a contingent encouraging her, Florence went back to running. In 1987, she placed second at the World Championships in the 200-meter race and was part of the winning relay team. On October 10, 1987, she and Al were married.

At this time, Griffith-Joyner took on a new resolve to be the best. Now sporting her trademark one-legged running suit, Joyner won Olympic trials handily, breaking a number of world records. In the 1988 Olympics, "Flo Jo," as she was now called, won three gold medals and one silver. She also took home the 1988 Sullivan Award.

Sadly, Joyner died unexpectantly in early 1999. Her young daughter, Mary, is said to be training to run in her mother's footsteps.

Suggested Activity

Running: Take turns running sprints and relays. How do the students compare to Joyner's times?

The Greatest

Few athletes make it to the professional leagues, and even fewer became famous in their sport. It is a rare athlete, indeed, who gains not only international fame but is considered by some to be the greatest athlete of all time. One of these rare few is Wayne Gretzky.

Born in Brantford, Ontario, Canada, on January 26, 1961, Gretzky became a professional hockey player in 1978 at the age of seventeen. At the time, he played with the Indianapolis Racers of the World Hockey Association (WHA). He was traded to the Edmonton Oilers, also of the WHA, later in 1978. At the end of the season, the WHA disbanded and the Oilers became a part of the National Hockey League (NHL).

In 1980, Gretzky became the youngest player ever to win the Hart Memorial Trophy for the most valuable player in the NHL. He was twenty years old. He went on to win the award each year for the next seven seasons, and he won it again in 1989. Gretzky, wearing his trademark #99 uniform, led the Oilers to four Stanley Cup championships.

Wayne Gretzky

Gretzky holds a total of 50 records for his playing, more records than any athlete in any major sport. In his third year as a professional, he set records for goals, assists, and total points, becoming the first player to score 200 points in one season. In 1986, Gretzky had a record 163 assists and broke his own record with 215 season points. In 1989, he broke Gordie Howe's 1,850 career scoring record, and in 1994, his career goal record surpassed Howe's record of 801 goals.

In 1988, Gretzky was traded to the Los Angeles Kings, a move that many criticized because the Oilers were a championship team and the Kings a losing one. The move proved to be excellent for the Kings franchise and, in Gretzky's opinion, challenging and fulfilling for himself. The Kings played to sellout crowds, unheard of for the once little-noticed team. Suddenly, the Kings became a Los Angeles favorite and a Stanley Cup contender. The attention they brought to the sport with the direct assistance of Gretzky may have paved the way for a new team in the area, the Anaheim Mighty Ducks.

Gretzky completed his run with the Kings in the 1995–1996 season, and he played out the season with the St. Louis Blues. Then, as a free agent, he signed with the championship New York Rangers, beginning with the 1996–1997 season. Fittingly, #99 retired in '99. It is no wonder that people call him "The Greatest."

Suggested Activities

Reading: Read excerpts from Gretzky's book entitled *Gretzky: An Autobiography*, co-written with Rick Reilly (HarperCollins, 1990).

Physical Education: Learn the basics of street hockey and play the game. You can simply wear tennis shoes instead of skates.

Canada: In Canada, hockey is the national sport in much the same way that baseball is in the United States. Learn more about Canada's relationship to hockey and what the trade to an American team might have meant to Gretzky.

Steffi Graf

On June 14, 1969, Steffi Graf was born in Mannheim, West Germany. At age thirteen, she began playing tennis professionally. By the time she was twenty-one, she was virtually unbeatable.

Graf is particularly renowned for her fierce forehand hit. Other players claim that the power with which she can hit the tennis ball is sometimes frightening. For her part, Graf says that the sport always came naturally to her. "It's just in you as a child. You pick up the racket, and you just play." She has certainly done that in a very big way.

Graf's career, which was still in full swing at the close of the century, is peppered with outstanding achievements. In 1982, she handily won West Germany's eighteen-and-under tennis championship. Four years later, in 1986 (at age sixteen), Graf won her first professional tournament, defeating superstar Chris Evert to win the Family Circle Cup. One year later, she won the French Open, her first Grand Slam singles championship.

Success after success followed. In 1988, Graf became the first woman to win the Grand Slam by taking the Australian Open, French Open, U.S. Open, and Wimbledon in the same year. At Wimbledon, Graf defeated Martina Navratilova, who was the reigning champion and also Graf's idol. The win was thrilling. It marked a new wave in tennis. Evert and Navratilova were completing their long careers while Graf was becoming the new champion.

That same year, Graf also participated in the summer Olympic Games, taking the gold in women's tennis. She also won Wimbledon, the U.S. Open, and the Australian Open in 1989.

In 1990, Graf lost two months of play due to an injured hand; she still won the Australian Open that year, though. By 1992, she was again in great form, winning Wimbledon even while losing her number-one ranking to the player she saw as her fiercest competition, Monica Seles.

Tragedy struck in 1993 when a crazed Graf fan stabbed Seles at a tennis match, hoping to aid Graf. Seles dropped out of the game for three years, too injured and traumatized to play. The memory of her connection with the crime still disturbs Graf. However, she did win the U.S. Open, Wimbledon, and the French Open in 1993. Another Australian Open win followed in 1994.

1995 was an excellent year for Graf as she took Wimbledon, the French Open, and finally the U.S. Open, defeating Seles. The U.S. Open offered particularly dramatic play that year, and it became Graf's eighteenth Grand Slam title. Three more titles followed in 1996 with French Open, U.S. Open, and Wimbledon wins. Although injuries and pains began to mount, Graf also won her twenty-second Grand Slam title in 1999 when she took the French Open once more.

For now, Graf continues to play the sport that she began to dominate almost as soon as she started to play. She certainly will be remembered as one of the greatest athletes of the century.

Suggested Activities

Tennis: Learn the fundamentals and rules of tennis. Hold a classroom tennis tournament.

Statistics: Compare Graf's statistics to those of other tennis greats such as Navratilova, Evert, and Seles.

Fonda and Fitness

Although her name has not always been linked with athletics, Jane Fonda came to the forefront in the eighties as the leading fitness guru. Her line of aerobic workout videos became some of the biggest selling tapes of the decade, and her fit, trim physique seemed to indicate that her methods could work.

Jane Fonda was born in 1937 in New York City to film star Henry Fonda and his wife. She attended Vassar College before pursuing acting with the renowned coach, Lee Strasberg, of the Actors Studio. In 1960, she was named most promising actress by the New York Drama Critics' Circle as a result of her Broadway debut in *There Was a Little Girl.* She went on to make motion pictures, including the critically acclaimed *A Walk on the Wild Side* (1962), *Sunday in New York* (1964), and *Klute* (1971), for which she won an Academy Award for best actress. In 1978, Fonda formed her own production company, IPC Films, and she won another best actress Academy Award for her role in *Coming Home,* which IPC produced. The company also made the critically acclaimed films *The China Syndrome* (1979) and *On Golden Pond* (1981), in which Fonda co-starred with her father.

Despite the wealth of work and accomplishments that came before, the eighties remember Fonda for one particular reason: fitness. Fonda was at the forefront of the growing aerobics craze. Running, weight lifting, and general calisthenics were the exercises of choice in prior times, but a budding interest in aerobic fitness was nurtured and blossomed under Fonda's endorsement. She produced and was featured in a number of instructional videos that sold phenomenally well throughout the decade. She also published *Jane Fonda's Workout Book* in 1981, one of the top books of the time. Hundreds of copycat videos followed those made by Fonda, but hers usually held strong at the top of the market.

Of course, with Fonda's success came the eventual backlash. A number of critics from the ranks of fitness experts objected to Fonda's lack of credentials, high impact routines, difficult maneuvers, and more. Some even asserted that her videos could be dangerous, causing too much strain on the body. However, no major difficulties were ever proven, and the videos continue to sell today. The public has learned that exercise regimes are personal choices, and that what works for one may not be in the best interest of another. Fonda kept up with this perspective by producing a variety of videos which utilized different approaches and were intended for different audiences. She even produced a program specifically for pregnant women.

Today Fonda is married to billionaire mogul Ted Turner. Her last films were *Old Gringo* in 1989 and *Stanley and Iris* in 1990. After marrying Turner in 1991, Fonda declared that she was giving up acting. While her videos can still be found, modern times see new crazes like Tae Bo taking their place, and new fitness gurus like High Voltage leading the way.

Suggested Activities

Video: As a class, create your own workout video. Develop a workout routine, rehearse it, set it to music, and tape it for class use or for fundraising purposes. Use Fonda's tapes to give you ideas on how such videos are made.

Vietnam: Fonda is also known as a former antiwar activist, and in 1972 she was dubbed "Hanoi Jane." Learn about Fonda's perspective and her activities in North Vietnam. Also learn about her 1973 marriage to fellow activist Tom Hayden-their political leanings and the life they lived together.

The Heart of the Matter

The human heart took on some different forms during the 1980s. Here are two of them.

A retired dentist from Seattle, Washington, became the first human recipient of a permanent artificial heart in the winter of 1982. Barney Clark's own heart was failing rapidly, so a surgical team headed by Dr. William C. DeVries at the University of Utah Medical Center replaced Clark's damaged heart with the Jarvik-7, an artificial heart created by inventor Robert Jarvik.

The Jarvik-7 is a mechanical heart that is powered by an air compressor that remains outside of the body. Two plastic hoses connect the compressor to the heart. The heart was first tested on animals and approved by the United States Food and Drug Administration (FDA) for human use.

Barney Clark

Clark lived for 112 days after the surgery, recovering enough to walk and move about. Eventually, though, his other organs failed and he died in March of 1983. Doctors attempted the surgery once more in 1984, this time with 54-year-old William J. Schroeder. Schroeder experienced a number of strokes after receiving the heart, and although he was able to leave the hospital and continue to live for 620 days, he died as well.

Many doctors became concerned over the dangers associated with the Jarvik-7, particularly the possibility of stroke. In 1990, the FDA withdrew its approval for the artificial heart.

An artificial heart had been used many years earlier but only as a temporary replacement. It was placed in the chest of a human patient for sixty hours in 1969 in order to keep the patient's blood circulating until a suitable human heart became available for transplanting.

In 1984, another kind of heart transplant was attempted, this time from animal to human. Doctors at Loma Linda University Medical Center in California transplanted the heart of a baboon into a baby born with a fatal heart defect. The baby lived for three weeks. The transplant also registered a great deal of controversy in the medical community, particularly since it was so experimental.

Suggested Activities

Science: Learn about the functioning of a heart. Draw diagrams of a normal, healthy heart. Also research diseases of the heart.

Research: Find out about the medical advances made in the 1990s concerning the human heart. What has been accomplished? What questions or concerns have been raised?

Discussion: Discuss the controversies of using animals for medical research and of scientific experimentation on human beings. These topics are likely to generate strong opinions, and it is usually best for the teacher to remain neutral.

Women in Space

The 1980s brought groundbreaking changes for women in many areas, but perhaps none as great as space. Three notable women changed the face of the space program forever.

Sally Ride

In 1983, Dr. Sally Ride became the first American woman to travel into space. She was born in Los Angeles, California, in 1951, and she graduated from Stanford University with a degree in English and another in astrophysics. She continued her study of astrophysics, earning both master's and doctoral degrees in the field. In 1978, she was chosen to be a part of NASA's astronaut training program, and in 1983, she made her famous flight aboard the space shuttle *Challenger* as the mission specialist. After her flight in 1983, she became a national hero.

Dr. Judith A. Resnick, an engineer and astronaut, was the second American woman in space. She made her first shuttle flight aboard the *Discovery* in September of 1984. Her second shuttle flight was as a mission specialist on the ill-fated tenth voyage of the *Challenger*. Resnick was born in 1949 in Akron, Ohio. She received her degree in engineering from Carnegie Tech University and earned a Ph.D. in electrical engineering from the University of Maryland in 1977. She was an accomplished classical pianist.

Christa McAuliffe

Another famous space traveler in connection with the *Challenger* was Christa McAuliffe. She was the first civilian ever selected to fly in space. Born Sharon Christa Corrigan in 1948, McAuliffe graduated from Framingham State College in 1970 and from Bowie State College in 1978 with a master's degree. She was a social studies teacher at Concord High School in Concord, New Hampshire, when she was selected by NASA from 11,000 applicants to be the first teacher in space.

McAuliffe began a diary at the time she was chosen in order to record her experiences for posterity. She planned to write about the journey while she was experiencing it; however, on January 28, 1986, after less than 80 seconds in flight, the *Challenger* exploded, killing all seven crew members. (See page 52.) Since the explosion, McAuliffe's fame has continued to spread, scholarships have been established in her honor, and schools and libraries around the nation have been named for her.

Suggested Activities

Read: Read *Sally Ride, Astronaut: An American First* by June Behrens (Children Press, 1984) and *The Story of the Challenger Disaster* by Zachary Kent (Childrens Press, 1986).

Other Notable Women: Other women worth mentioning in terms of the space program include Dr. Mae C. Jemison, Dr. Kathryn Sullivan, and Lt. Col. Eileen Collins. Research to learn about each of them and their contributions to the space program.

Famous Firsts: As a class, brainstorm for the names of women throughout history who have accomplished "famous firsts." A number of such women are named throughout the many pages of this book.

Discuss: President Ronald Reagan first suggested sending a teacher into space. Ask the students to discuss why they think he made this suggestion and why NASA agreed. Also ask them if they would like to be selected for space flight and why or why not.

Space Shuttles

In the sixties, scientists learned how expensive space travel could be. The expendable booster rockets used to launch satellites for commercial and government use were expensive. A reusable spacecraft, together with launch facilities, mission control, and a system of tracking and data control satellites, would create a new Space Transportation System (STS).

These new spacecraft had to be designed for safety, performance, endurance, and longevity. There are three main components to the shuttle: the orbiter, the external tank, and the solid fuel rocket boosters. The orbiter, which looks like a delta wing fighter, has a wing span of 78 feet (23.79 m) and is 122 feet (37.2 m) long. In its launch phase it is a rocket, in orbit it is a spacecraft, and in re-entry it is a hypersonic glider. The orbiter contains living space for the astronauts, a large cargo bay, and the engine compartment. The design allows for more crew members than previous spacecrafts and enables the astronauts to bring home large quantities of weighty cargo. There is plenty of room for a variety of work, such as satellite repair, experimentation, the construction of space stations, and deployment of satellites. In theory each orbiter could make one hundred voyages, although the engines would only last through about fifty-five launches. The first orbiter, *Enterprise*, was ready in 1977. It was used solely for drop tests from a Boeing 747 Jumbo Jet, which tested its ability to land after space travel.

An external tank holds cylinders of liquid hydrogen and oxygen to fuel the orbiter's three main engines. Two solid fuel rocket boosters are used to help propel the orbiter to the upper atmosphere. Each one produces 2.65 million pounds (1.20 kg) of thrust.

On April 12, 1981, the first operational shuttle, *Columbia*, piloted by astronauts John W. Young and Robert L. Crippen, went into orbit. They circled the Earth thirty-six times over a period of more than two days. During this flight, the astronauts deployed scientific equipment and ran a variety of tests checking out the abilities of the shuttle.

The sixth shuttle flight in April of 1983 was the first for the orbiter *Challenger*. When *Discovery* was launched in 1984, the crew included Charles Walker of the McDonnell Douglas Corporation, the first person from industry assigned to a shuttle mission. In 1985, U.S. senator Jake Garn flew on the shuttle and took part in medical experiments. The fourth orbiter, *Atlantis*, made its debut for the twenty-first shuttle flight in October of 1985.

Challenger successfully completed nine flights; but on its tenth (the twenty-fifth shuttle mission altogether), in January of 1986, it exploded less than 80 seconds after takeoff. (See page 52.) The space shuttle program was halted until the problem could be completely remedied.

The program resumed with shuttle mission 26, completed October 3, 1988, by *Discovery*.

Suggested Activities

Space Flight: Learn about other space vehicles of the 1980s, such as *Voyager*. How were they constructed? What did they do? How were they different from those that came before? Also find out about plans for the future of space flight and space exploration.

Read: There are many excellent resources about the space shuttle program. Two of them are *Space Shuttle* by N.S. Barrett (Franklin Watts, 1985) and *I Want to Fly the Shuttle* by David Baker (Rourke Enterprises, 1988). Read them as well as others to learn more.

Building: Construct models of the space shuttle.

Astronaut: Learn about Guion Bluford, the first African American to fly into space. He was the mission specialist on the third flight of the *Challenger*.

Disaster in the Air

"Oh, I have slipped the surly bonds of earth, . . . put out my hand, and touched the face of God." When President Ronald Reagan quoted Canadian World War II pilot John Gillespie Magee, Jr., who was killed in action at the age of nineteen, he referred not to Magee but to the seven members of the space shuttle *Challenger*'s flight crew who died in a tragic explosion just over a minute after liftoff on January 28, 1986. Thousands of onlookers, including family and friends of the crew, watched the shuttle blow apart nine miles (14.5 kilometers) in the sky, and millions more saw the scene on their television screens as it was replayed throughout the next several days and weeks. The American space program had known tragedy but nothing on this order. Moreover, it seemed that people had come to take space flight, already in existence for more than two decades, almost for granted. The explosion of the craft brought waves of shock and disbelief.

The tenth flight of the *Challenger* was particularly noteworthy since its crew included the first civilian ever selected to fly into space. Chosen from among 11,000 applicants, Christa McAuliffe was a high school social studies teacher from Concord, New Hampshire, who was selected to be the ambassador to educators and schoolchildren from around the nation. Many students watched the liftoff on televisions in their schools. Around the nation, the spirits of the children fell as the reality of what had happened sank in. Teachers and students at McAuliffe's own school were sent home just an hour after the tragedy occurred.

Lifting off at 11:38 A.M., the shuttle no longer existed by 11:40. A gas leak from a faulty seal in a solid-fuel booster rocket caused the explosion. Recordings of voices from the crew cockpit confirm that the crew knew there was a problem, but only briefly. The pilot said, "Uh-oh," just before the explosion.

In addition to McAuliffe, the crew included Commander Michael J. Smith, Commander Francis "Dick" Scobee, Dr. Judith A. Resnik, Dr. Ronald E. McNair, Lieutenant Colonel Ellison S. Onizuka, and Gregory B. Jarvis. Jarvis was an engineer from the Hughes Aircraft Company, and, like McAuliffe, this was his first shuttle flight.

The immediate cause of the fiery explosion was a defect in one of the solid-fuel booster rockets, but in the months that followed, reports also showed that pressure on NASA to launch the shuttles was partly responsible for the tragedy. Some engineers had recommended that the flight be delayed, but these recommendations were overlooked in order to get the shuttle into space. After the accident, the space shuttle program was completely shut down until all such problems and potential hazards could be remedied. On September 29, 1988, two-and-a-half years after the *Challenger* explosion, the space shuttle *Discovery* was launched without incident. The nation breathed a collective sigh of relief.

Suggested Activity

Read: Read more about the explosion of the *Challenger* and what it meant to the space program. One good resource is listed on page 50.

The Technological Home and Office

The average American home of the eighties differed quite a bit from the same home in the seventies, and technology was the reason. Suddenly it seemed there were new technologies to handle a variety of tasks. Answering machines took phone messages, videocassette recorders (VCRs) taped television shows when people were not home to watch them, cable television broadened the spectrum of television viewing options, compact discs (CDs) enhanced sound for the listener of recorded music, and personal computers rapidly became an exciting new source of entertainment and productivity. Perhaps most significant and influential in the technological advances of the decade were the VCR and the personal computer.

VCRs—VCRs brought about a revolution in the entertainment industry. Previously, people's choice of films was limited to what could be seen in theaters or the occasional few that were screened on network television. Children of the middle decades can recall special television events when popular movies such as *The Wizard of Oz* were broadcast annually. With the advent of VCRs, people could buy or rent video tapes of movies and watch them whenever they chose. They could also record any movie or show from television to watch at their leisure. Some even began watching a show on one channel while taping one on another. With the dawn of the VCR came a new line of stores that sold and rented videos. This became one of the fastest growing industries of the 1980s.

Initially developed in the late fifties and early sixties, VCR technology grew from the need of television studios for a reliable method of recording programs for viewing in different time zones or for repeat usage. These early systems were far too complex and expensive for home use, however. In 1975 Sony Corporation introduced its Betamax based on the system used by stations and networks. Matsushita Electric Industrial Corporation quickly released a competing system called Video Home System, or VHS. When the VHS system was adopted by the leading American television manufacturer, popularity of the Betamax waned. The VCR industry boomed throughout the eighties.

PCs—The personal computer also took off in popularity throughout the decade. Although in 1979 only 325,000 Americans had personal computers in their homes, by 1984 the number of owners had climbed to 15 million.

The first home computers were used primarily for entertainment with such games as Space Invaders and Pac Man. Advances in microchip technology and the availability of affordable peripherals like modems and user-friendly software led to growing awareness of the computer's usefulness, particularly to students. By 1985, students had become the largest users of personal computers.

While the prices of both VCRs and personal computers have dropped over time, VCRs are usually more affordable for the average family, while personal computers, still relatively expensive, are often out of reach. However, most schools have computers so that students are exposed to them before entering into the business world, where they are a staple.

Suggested Activities

Viewing: Watch portions of *The Desk Set*, a classic Hepburn-Tracy movie that comically demonstrates the advent of computers—at that time huge, monstrous things—in the business world.

Survey: Have the students conduct surveys concerning the number of VCRs and personal computers in homes in their neighborhoods (or, perhaps, in extended families). Graph the results.

Challenge: Test students' basic understanding of the operation of VCRs and personal computers. Conduct challenges where students test themselves against one another.

Technology: Learn about the technological operations of the VCR and the personal computer.

Uncle Shelby

Not everyone knows his name, but many adults and children know his work. The man is Shel Silverstein, and he was one of the most successful writers of the eighties.

Shelby Silverstein was born in Chicago, Illinois, in 1932. In the 1950s, he served with the United States armed forces in Korea and Japan. In 1956, he became a writer and cartoonist for *Playboy* magazine. His first book, *Now Here's My Plan: A Book of Futilities*, was published in 1960. More books followed quickly: *Uncle Shelby's ABZ Book: A Primer for Tender Minds* in 1961, *A Playboy's Teevee Jeebies* in 1963, and *Uncle Shelby's Story of Lafcadio, the Lion Who Shot Back*, a book for children, in 1963. Huge success came with his 1964 publication, *The Giving Tree*, although it nearly was not published and sold slowly once it was. Silverstein's publisher thought that it had limited appeal and was too sad for children and too simple for adults. Initial sales were mild, but once churches and other groups started sharing it for its allegoric message, the book caught on and began to skyrocket.

Shel Silverstein

Many other books followed, including *Where the Sidewalk Ends* in 1974, *The Missing Piece* in 1976, and *A Light in the Attic* in 1981. Each of these books proved hugely successful with both children and adults. *Where the Sidewalk Ends* had sold a million hardback copies by 1980, 250,000 of them in that year alone. *A Light in the Attic*, published as a children's book, became a breakthrough publication when it reached the top of the adult nonfiction charts in 1981. In 1985, Silverstein's *Attic* had reached an extraordinary 112 weeks on the *New York Times* bestseller list.

Silverstein was also a playwright, composer, and lyricist. His songs include "The Unicorn Song" and "The Boa Constrictor Song." They have been recorded by Johnny Cash, Dr. Hook, the Irish Rovers, and Jerry Lee Lewis. He received an Academy Award nomination for music he composed for the film *Postcards From the Edge*. Renowned actor Richard Dreyfuss starred in his one-act play, *The Lady and the Tiger*.

Although Silverstein once gave a number of interviews, over the past two decades he withdrew from public communication. He wished to communicate through his writings. As Silverstein said, "I'll keep on communicating, but only my way." He died in 1999.

Suggested Activities

Read: Select a variety of poems from Silverstein's poetry collection or read one of his books for children. Talk about what you read and heard.

Writing: Write poems or stories in the style of Shel Silverstein.

Illustrating: Silverstein developed his own style to illustrate his stories. Select a Silverstein poem or humorous song to illustrate in your own style.

Alice Walker

One of the most renowned authors of the eighties was the writer Alice Walker. Born Alice Malsenior Walker in Eatonton, Georgia, in 1944, Walker always had a love for writing. She attended Spelman and Sarah Lawrence colleges, where she fostered her talents. In 1964, she wrote her first volume of poetry in one week. Entitled *Once*, it was published four years later in 1968.

Many of Walker's personal experiences have found their way into her books, including an unwanted pregnancy in her college years and a trip to Africa. The themes of her novels vary and deal with such wide-ranging topics as love, suicide, and civil rights. Most of her writing portrays poor and oppressed African-American women in the early part of the twentieth century.

Walker's best-known novel, *The Color Purple,* was published in 1982. It won both the American Book Award and the Pulitzer Prize. The book was critically acclaimed because of its well developed characters and lyrical language which captured the people and the time. In 1985, her novel was made into a film by popular director Stephen Spielberg. Controversy surrounded Spielberg's making of the film since many people thought that such a story could only be told accurately by an African American. The film was a success, but many believe that the lack of Oscars given to the movie and director at the Academy Awards was due to the controversy. The movie also marked the film debut of a rising talk-show host named Oprah Winfrey and a stand-up comedian named Whoopi Goldberg. Another book by Walker, *The Same River Twice: Honoring the Difficult* (1996), tells the author's perspective on making the film.

Other works by Alice Walker include *The Third Life of Grange Copeland* (1970), *Meridian* (1976), *The Temple of My Familiar* (1989), and *Possessing the Secret of Joy* (1992). Her poetry volumes include *Revolutionary Petunias and Other Poems* (1973) and *Goodnight, Willie Lee, I'll See You in the Morning* (1979). She has also published two essay collections, entitled *In Search of Our Mothers' Gardens: Womanist Prose* (1983) and *Living by the Word* (1988).

Over time, Walker has received numerous awards and honors for her writing and is today considered to be one of the greatest living authors, as well as an important writer of the twentieth century.

Besides her writing, Walker has also been extensively involved in a variety of causes close to her heart. These include most especially civil and women's rights. Her passion concerning both movements can clearly be seen in her publications.

Suggested Activities

Poetry: Read some poems by Alice Walker and study her style of writing. Then attempt to write a poem that mimics her style. Is it easy or challenging to write as she does?

Colors: Purple has special significance in Walker's Pulitzer Prize-winning novel. As a class, discuss the various symbolic meanings of colors as used in speech and writing. Create a color chart that includes words showing what the colors sometimes represent.

Causes: Walker often included causes that are important to her in her writing. Choose a cause that is important to you. Then draft the outline of a story that incorporates your cause.

Stephen King

One of the most prolific and popular authors of the eighties, Stephen King's name has become synonymous with horror and fantasy fiction.

Stephen King was born in Portland, Maine, in 1947. He has always had a passionate love of storytelling, and, in fact, he wrote his first story at the tender age of seven. At eighteen he became a published author when he sold his first writing to a magazine.

King graduated from the University of Maine at Orono in 1970, and his publishing career took off shortly thereafter. His first novel was published in 1973. *Carrie* tells the story of a young woman who exacts revenge on her cruel classmates by using her telekinetic powers, which allow her to move objects without physically touching them. The novel was enormously successful, selling millions of copies. In 1975, the book was made into a motion picture starring Sissy Spacek. It has become a cult classic.

More books and subsequent films followed. *The Shining* (1976) tells of an ordinary family that moves into a secluded mountain resort in the dead of winter. Some type of madness overcomes the father, who then attacks his family. This, too, was made into a successful film, starring Jack Nicholson. "Here's Johnny," a line from the film (taken from *The Tonight Show,* starring Johnny Carson), quickly became a part of the language of popular culture.

Other novels include *The Stand* (1978), *Christine* (1983), *It* (1986), *Misery* (1987), *Needful Things* (1991), *Insomnia* (1994), *Rose Madder* (1995), and a six-part serial, *The Green Mile* (1996). The latter was written in serial form in the hopes that it would heighten suspense. King has also published a number of short story collections, such as *Night Shift* (1978) and *Skeleton Crew* (1985).

No book written by King has been financially unsuccessful. His books immediately top the charts after publication, and die-hard fans wait hungrily for his next publication. King is known for his diligence as a writer. It is said that he sits down daily to write, and that is one of the reasons why he is so prolific. He is also a natural storyteller, although he has certainly sharpened his skills by utilizing them so continuously.

Not all of King's writing is horror-based. Many people are surprised to learn that the poignant coming-of-age film *Stand By Me* is based on a King novella. King has also published writing under the pseudonym Richard Bachman.

Because of Stephen King's influence and popularity, horror and fantasy fiction have become mainstays of late twentieth century literature.

Suggested Activities

Writing: In honor of Stephen King, write original horror stories. Try to do as King does, turning ordinary people and situations into terrifying ones.

Reading: Read a Stephen King story. (Check first for appropriateness.) Then make a movie poster as though the story were going to be made into a film.

I.M. Pei

Perhaps the best architect of the latter twentieth century, Ieoh Ming Pei was born on April 26, 1917, in Guangzhou (Canton), China. In 1935, he immigrated to the United States. Pei studied architecture at the Massachusetts Institute of Technology as well as at Harvard University. He then taught at Harvard from 1945 to 1948.

Pei's style has always been noted for its innovative sense, while at the same time it remains classically elegant and functions with the height of efficiency. The architect's breathtaking style is perhaps surpassed only by his tremendous prolificacy.

Louvre Pyramid

In 1956, Pei established his own firm, I.M. Pei & Partners. The firm became responsible for many of the most significant municipal and corporate structures of the middle- to late- twentieth century in both the United States and abroad. Among the designs Pei has created with his firm are the famous Place Ville-Marie (1961) in Montreal, Canada; the Mile High Center (1955) in Denver, Colorado; and the John Hancock Tower (1973) in Boston, Massachusetts. The last is a striking building covered with blue-green mirrored glass intended to reflect the picturesque Copley Square below it. Also of significance is the East Building of the National Gallery of Art (1978) in Washington, D.C., a trapezoidal structure with triangular wings, skylights, and protruding, knife-like fins.

Pei's largest projects to date are the Jacob K. Javits Convention Center (1980–1986) constructed in New York City and the rebuilding program for the famous Louvre museum (1984–1996) of Paris, France. The Louvre project was an extremely controversial one. Many Parisians felt that the historic museum should remain exactly as it had been and that Pei's addition was a garish inclusion. Others believed that the old and new styles contrasted beautifully. In the end, the building was constructed, generally to glowing reviews.

For reasons of his style, his prolificacy, his international acclaim, and his significant skill, I.M. Pei is considered to be one of the leading artists of the twentieth century.

Suggested Activities

Architecture: Collect a variety of building supplies, including cardboard boxes, index paper, scissors, glue, craft sticks, and more. In small groups, create three-dimensional architectural designs. Ask a teacher or the principal to come into the classroom to judge the groups' work. Award the best structure the I.M. Pei Award of Architectural Excellence.

Mathematics: Architecture requires precise mathematical equations concerning area, circumference, and other matters of size. Physics also plays an important role in construction. Learn more about the necessary math for a career in architecture. It might also prove wise to take a moment at this time to explore how math can aid a variety of interesting and profitable professions.

David Hockney

There were many popular artists throughout the eighties, and some are likely to stay popular only within that realm. The work of a few, however, will be remembered throughout time. One such artist is David Hockney.

Born in England in 1937, Hockney is a renowned painter, draftsman, photographer, and set designer. He is known for his distinctive prints and drawings, his skillful portraits of contemporary individuals, and his satirical paintings. In the 1960s, he worked most often with bright colors and a primitive style. His subject matter of the time was primarily popular culture.

Perhaps best known among Hockney's work is the series he did of Los Angeles swimming pools and the people who could be found in and around them. *A Bigger Splash* (1967) is the best known of this group. Today it hangs in the Tate Gallery of London.

About his paintings of water, Hockney wrote, "It is a formal problem to represent water, to describe water, because it can be anything. It can be any color, it's movable, and it has no set visual description." The painting of water fascinated the artist.

By the end of the sixties, Hockney's style had changed to a more naturalistic one, particularly in his portraits. His works of this time are not expressly realistic; however, they do provide a heightened sense of their subjects, a sort of hyper-realism. These works were generally created with flat acrylic paints and finely drawn lines.

When Hockney turned next to set design for operatic productions, he became a huge success in the industry. His designs for both the Glyndebourne Opera in England and the Metropolitan Opera in New York City gained both popular and critical acclaim.

In 1982, Hockney published a book entitled *David Hockney Photographs*. This book is a partial autobiography coupled with a discussion of the medium of photography.

A style of photography most often associated with David is called "joiners." This is a type of photo collage. Taking numerous photographs that captured small parts of a large scene, Hockney pieced the photos together, creating a skewed realistic image. One classic example of Hockney's composite Polaroid images is 1982's *Henry Moore*.

Suggested Activities

Photography: In small groups, if you have the means, take photographs of scenes to create a composite work of art in the style of David Hockney.

Art: Hockney was fascinated with painting water. Using watercolors, paint scenes of natural bodies of water, puddles of water, swimming pools, or bath tubs—any scene depicting water. Experiment with ways to show movement in the water. Try different perspectives of the same particular scene.

Portraits: Painting portraits is a tricky business. Try this to learn how they are done. Choose a large-sized photograph of an individual from a magazine. Cut the photo in half vertically down the center of the face. Glue one half to a sheet of drawing paper. Using the half face as a guide, draw in the missing half. (Note: Faces are not completely symmetrical. There are some variations from side to side.)

Maya Lin

The artist and architect Maya Lin was born in Athens, Ohio, on October 5, 1959. Her parents were immigrants from China who both served on the faculty of Ohio University. Lin spent a great deal of time there while she was growing up. She herself attended Yale University.

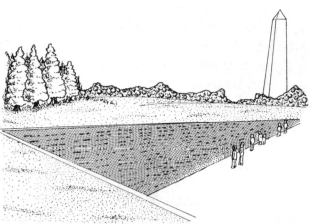

The Vietnam Veterans Memorial Fund, a nonprofit organization begun by a group of Vietnam veterans, wanted to build a memorial at the nation's capital to veterans of the Vietnam War. In the fall of 1980 they announced a competition to design the new memorial. They asked for entries that would pay tribute to the veterans in a meaningful way, and they wanted the names of all American Vietnam War soldiers who were killed or missing placed on the memorial in some way. All entries were to be sent on two-by-four foot (60 cm x 120 cm) panels. By the deadline on March 31, 1981, the organization had received a total of 1,421 entries.

When all of the entries were set up for display, they stretched for more than a mile (1.6 kilometers). The names on the entries were replaced with numbers, and the judging began. The judges were prominent architects and landscape designers, and they did their judging over the course of one week.

Entry number 1,026 was not done in the same style as most of the others. It was submitted by Maya Lin, who was a twenty-one year old undergraduate art student at the time. She had only recently decided to be an architect, and her work was somewhat smudged and lacked the professional quality of many of the others. However, the judges said that they were haunted by her design. The panel of judges narrowed the enormous field of entries to thirty-nine and then to eighteen finalists. Finally, in early May of 1981, a winner was chosen. It was entry number 1,026.

Maya Lin became an instant celebrity. Not only did she gain fame through the use of her design in an enduring national memorial but she was paid $20,000 which she used to further her education. Lin's design was very simple. Two walls of black marble delved into the earth, meeting at their highest points. Together, they comprised two sides of a triangle. The walls descended into the earth rather than being placed above it. On the face of the walls were carved the nearly 58,000 names. Public opinion was very positive about her design at first, but as publicity spread, some began to protest. Several wanted a traditional looking memorial, such as a statue, while others were troubled that an individual of Asian descent had designed a memorial for a war fought in Southeast Asia. The memorial was placed in the Constitution Gardens of the Mall on Capitol Hill, between the Lincoln and Washington Memorials.

Today, Maya Lin's tribute to the Vietnam War veterans has become one of the most famous landmarks in the United States. Lin herself went on to receive her master's degree in architecture from Yale University and an honorary doctorate of fine arts degree from Yale as well. In 1988, she received the Presidential Design Award for her design of the Vietnam Veterans Memorial.

Suggested Activities

Memorials: Learn about the other memorials in Washington, D.C.: what they look like, how they came to be, and what they represent.

Architect: Choose a topic that you believe should be memorialized. Design a memorial in tribute.

Michael Jackson

Michael Jackson

Born to a musical family in Gary, Indiana, in 1958, Michael Joseph Jackson came to be arguably the biggest pop music star of all time. His music career began at the age of five when he and his four brothers started performing under their father's management as the Jackson Five. Jackson became the group's lead singer and dancer, delighting fans with his intricate footwork and energetic vocals. In the 1970s, the Jackson Five became the main characters in a Saturday morning cartoon series for children. In 1976, they changed their name to the Jacksons. By the late seventies, Michael Jackson had left the group.

Michael Jackson recorded his first solo album in 1972, *Got to Be There*. He established himself as a solo artist in 1979 with *Off the Wall*, a highly successful album. But it was the release of *Thriller*, the largest selling album of all time, in 1982 that propelled him to superstardom and unparalleled success. The album sold about forty million copies internationally and produced a number of chart-topping single hits, including the title song, "Beat It," and "Billie Jean." The album also introduced a new type of music video, longer than the standard three- to four-minute version. Jackson's video for the title song was a minimovie thirteen minutes long. It included dialogue, prolonged dance segments, and special effects. Many other Jackson videos followed this lead, breaking new ground in the music video industry.

After *Thriller*, Jackson became a household name. Concerts around the world sold out instantly. People clambered to see the dancing and singing sensation, known for his amazing dance moves and his single, spangled glove. When he gave a rare performance during a televised tribute to Motown during the mid-eighties, millions of people tuned in just to see him. After the performance, dance legend Fred Astaire complimented Jackson on his exceptional dancing skills.

Jackson later said that Astaire's compliment was one of the most meaningful he had ever received, because dance had always been important to him. Jackson began developing his unique style at an early age by watching entertainers like James Brown and studying their movements. Although he found it frustrating when televised programs concentrated on singers' faces instead of feet, Jackson was able to mimic their styles and incorporate them into a style all his own.

Over the decade, the artist became known for other things as well, particularly the many plastic surgeries he underwent to alter and mold his features. Pictures of the man today are drastically different from the artist of the early eighties.

During the eighties, Jackson became the most popular and wealthiest entertainer in the world. In 1988, he published his autobiography, entitled *Moonwalk*. In 1994, he married the daughter of legendary rock musician, Elvis Presley. Lisa Marie Presley and Jackson soon divorced. Jackson's second wife, Debbie, a former nurse he met during his surgical procedures, gave birth to his first child, a son named Prince, early in 1997. The couple's daughter, Paris, arrived in 1998.

Suggested Activities

When I Grow Up: Michael Jackson was a performer almost from the time he was born. Write about your dreams if you could do anything you wished to do.

Moonwalk: Jackson became famous for a dance move called the Moonwalk. Learn to do the dance.

Whitney Houston

Whitney Houston

The youngest of three children, Whitney Houston was born in Newark, New Jersey, on August 9, 1963. At the age of eleven, she gave her first musical performance in front of an audience. It seemed just moments from then that she was a superstar.

Born to John and Cissy Houston, Whitney learned early how to perform. She was born with an extraordinary voice, but her mother, a professional singer, taught her how to use it. She first performed for her church, the New Hope Baptist Church, where her mother was choir director. Houston began touring with her mother after that, performing backup vocals. While on stage, she drew the attention of talent scouts who began offering her concert bookings. She also received many modeling offers, and in her teens she appeared in a variety of magazines, such as *Seventeen*, *Cosmopolitan*, and *Glamour*. Houston appeared in small roles in some television situation comedies, such as *Gimme a Break* and *Silver Spoons*.

In 1983, the president of Arista Records, Clive Davis, signed Houston to a recording contract. He was the man behind such talent as Barry Manilow, Billy Joel, and Janis Joplin—all extremely successful recording artists. Davis believed so deeply in Houston's talent that the contract he gave to her included a clause stating that if he ever left Arista Records, she could go with him.

Houston's first album was painstakingly planned out, and the top producers and writers in the business were selected. It was two years in the making, but when *Whitney Houston* debuted on February 14, 1985, it quickly became the number one album on the music charts, producing hit after hit. Followed in 1987 by *Whitney*, Houston's success grew by leaps and bounds. The second album debuted at number one, the first album by a female artist to do so. Her song "I Wanna Dance With Somebody" went to the top of eight different charts.

Houston's beauty served to improve her career, arriving as she did with the great new medium of the eighties, the music video. Her videos received almost constant airplay, as did her songs on the radio.

With each of the first two albums, Houston received the highest honors in the music field, Grammy Awards and American Music Awards. She became known for her thanks to God during her acceptance speeches. Houston has always maintained that her talent is God-given, and her job is merely to use it.

Houston's success brought inevitable movie contracts and additional albums, each hugely successful. Throughout the eighties, she became one of the biggest superstars in the music industry, and her success continued unabated into the nineties.

Suggested Activities

Music: Listen to some of Houston's music. A good selection from her early years is called "Greatest Love of All," a song about believing in oneself. The video of the song also includes Houston's mother.

Family: Houston came from a supportive, musical family. Both her mother and her cousin, Dionne Warwick, led successful musical careers and helped her develop her own. Write about a talent shared in your family and what sort of business your family might be able to do together if they chose.

John Lennon

John Winston Lennon was born on October 9, 1940, in Liverpool, England. As a child Lennon preferred drawing and writing to studying. Because of his artistic talent, he was accepted as a student at the Liverpool Art College, where he pursued commercial art. At the age of sixteen, he organized his first band, called the Quarrymen, to play popular music. Their music was heavily influenced by the early stars of rock and roll like Little Richard, Jerry Lee Lewis, and Chuck Berry. In 1957, Lennon met Paul McCartney, who soon joined the group. Later, George Harrison and Ringo Starr (Richard Starkey) joined the group, and the name was changed to the Beatles.

John Lennon

In 1960, Lennon dropped out of art school to devote more time to his music. He and Paul McCartney were the creative forces behind the singles such as "I Want to Hold Your Hand," "Please, Please Me," and "Love Me Do" which brought worldwide success and fame to the group. Over the years their music matured, and they developed rich instrumentations. Their lyrics often reflected the turbulence and social issues of the times. Such albums as *Sergeant Pepper's Lonely Hearts Club Band* and *Abbey Road* are considered classics in rock. No group in the history of popular music reached the phenomenal success and fan appeal that the Beatles did in the sixties. In 1965, Queen Elizabeth II made Lennon and the other Beatles Members of the Order of the British Empire (MBE), a prestigious honor.

In 1968 John Lennon divorced his wife, Cynthia Powell. The following year he married Yoko Ono, a Japanese artist he met at an art show in 1966. Ono introduced herself to him simply by handing him a card that read "Breath." After their marriage, Lennon changed his middle name from Winston to Ono.

The Beatles' last live performance was in 1969, and in 1970 the band disbanded over creative differences. Even before the breakup of the group, Lennon was performing both as a solo artist and with Ono. Over the next decade, he continued to write and record his music, sometimes with a group called The Plastic Ono Band.

Lennon was a pacifist and a proponent of social causes. His songs "Give Peace a Chance" and "Imagine" became anthems of the movement calling for peace in the world during and after the Vietnam War. Lennon and Ono once staged a sit-in in the bed in their New York apartment, calling for peace while thousands outside their building gathered and sang "Give Peace a Chance."

While returning from a recording session with his wife on December 8, 1980, John Lennon was shot and killed by a twenty-five-year-old amateur guitarist named Mark David Chapman in front of the Dakota, the New York hotel where Lennon and Ono lived with their young son. Later that day, hundreds of fans gathered outside the building, singing "All You Need Is Love," another of Lennon's songs. Millions of people were shocked and grieved over the violent and untimely end of the musician who had spoken so eloquently for peace and love.

Sales of the *Double Fantasy* album by Lennon and Ono, released earlier in the year, skyrocketed after Lennon's death.

In the nineties, the three remaining Beatles did reunite to record new material, incorporating recordings Lennon had made prior to his death.

Suggested Activity

Listen and Write: Listen to a few of Lennon's songs in class, particularly his anthems of peace and love. Write your own anthem.

Madonna

When Madonna first hit the airwaves and video screen, critics were sure she would be a one-hit wonder. Yet as the decade drew to a close, she was one of the most recognizable women in the world and so much the celebrity that even other celebrities were dumbstruck upon meeting her. There is no one like Madonna.

Born Madonna Louise Veronica Ciccone in Bay City, Michigan, in 1958, Madonna took to dancing, singing, and acting when she was a child. She earned a dance scholarship to the University of Michigan, which she attended for two years. Upon leaving school, she went straight to New York to pursue a music career.

Once in New York, Madonna formed a band and began to write songs. Her first album, entitled *Madonna*, came out in 1983, producing three singles that reached the top of the charts in 1984. Fueling Madonna's success was the rise in video production and airplay, particularly through the new music channel, MTV (Music Television). Madonna was attractive, engaging, and a skilled dancer, but she had something else that set her apart from the crowd. Her distinctive style delighted young people while baffling the older generations. Video became as much a reason for Madonna's success as did her music.

Madonna's next albums, *Like a Virgin* (1984), *True Blue* (1986), and *Like a Prayer* (1989), were also enormously successful. With each new album release, Madonna's style has changed. She consistently seemed to reinvent herself, and that kept the audience intrigued and wanting more.

During the mid-eighties Madonna also took part in a short-lived marriage to actor Sean Penn. Madonna would later declare that Penn was the love of her life.

In 1992, Madonna published a highly controversial book entitled *Sex*. It contained explicit photographs and a no-holds-barred approach to the topic. Despite its one-hundred-dollar price tag, the book sold out its first printing of more than one million copies.

Another reason for Madonna's success is the hands-on approach she has taken to her career. In 1992, she made a contractual agreement with Time Warner, Inc., which allowed her to create her own publishing, record, and movie company. Through this deal as well as her record-breaking success, Madonna quickly became one of the world's wealthiest women.

The singer has also actively pursued a career in films. She earned critical acclaim for 1985's *Desperately Seeking Susan,* and in 1997, she earned a Golden Globe as best actress for her performance in the film version of *Evita.* In that year, Madonna also gave birth to a daughter, Lourdes. Those who know the performer say that having a child has changed her outlook. Indeed, her public image softened and became more spiritual. Surely time will tell which incarnation of the chameleon-like performer will endure.

Suggested Activity

Style: Madonna is known as much for her style as for her music. Her look seems to change dramatically with each passing year or recording. Just for fun, try creating several different styles of your own. On each of the head outlines on the next page, design a different look. Then create at least three different styles of clothes for the paperdoll. Are you as stylistically prolific as Madonna?

Madonna *(cont.)*

Are you as diverse a stylist as Madonna? Create a different stylistic look for each of the two head outlines below. Then design at least three distinct outfits for the paper doll.

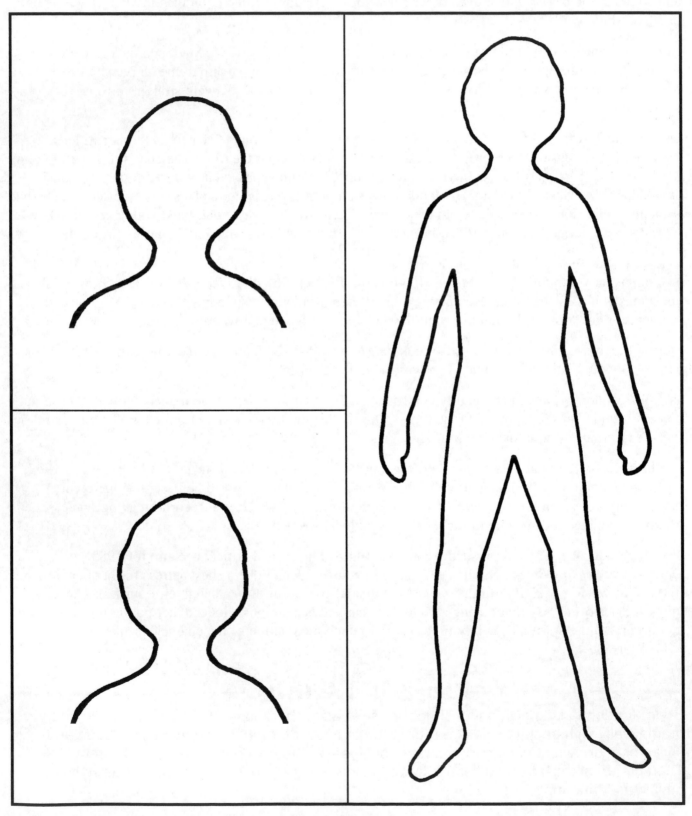

64

The Cos

On Thursday nights in the 1980s, millions of Americans turned on the television to *The Cosby Show*, one of the most popular shows of all time. For much of the 1980s, *The Cosby Show* was rated number one in the Nielsen rating system, demonstrating that people of all ages, races, and socio-economic backgrounds loved to watch "The Cos."

William Henry Cosby, Jr., was born in Philadelphia, Pennsylvania, in 1937. He began his career in entertainment as a stand-up comedian on the nightclub circuit while he was a student at Temple University. He began to record his comedy as well, making over twenty albums and reaching audiences around the world. People not only laughed at but were charmed by the family warmth and gentle, good-natured humor that pervaded his routines.

Bill Cosby

In 1965, Cosby became the first black actor to co-star in a prime-time dramatic series on television. The show *I Spy* ran until 1968. Cosby received three consecutive Emmys for his work. Cosby had become a star. He followed the show with a number of movie roles, including *Hickey and Boggs* in 1972 and *Uptown Saturday Night* in 1974. 1972 was also the year of Cosby's television debut as Fat Albert, the lead character in the cartoon series *Fat Albert and the Cosby Kids,* which Cosby produced and hosted. Fat Albert was a character Cosby had created for his comedy routines. Fat Albert became so popular with children that even Cosby's son, Ennis, is remembered as having been overjoyed to learn that his father was, in fact, Fat Albert. The character had another purpose, as well, serving as the basis for the doctoral dissertation in education that Cosby earned from the University of Massachusetts in 1977.

In 1984, Cosby's new situation comedy, *The Cosby Show*, debuted. It was an instant success, running until 1992 and continuing ever since in rerun syndication. The show was loosely based on Cosby's own experiences as the father of five children (one boy and four girls). The fame of the show made Cosby a star of the highest order, and he has frequently been counted as one of the wealthiest entertainers in the world.

Cosby also authored several books in the eighties, including *Fatherhood* in 1986, *Time Flies* in 1987, and *Love and Marriage* in 1989. His books are filled with the easily recognizable Cosby humor.

Other television series followed *The Cosby Show*, but none matched the phenomenal success of the show from the eighties. Early in 1997, Cosby's only son was killed by a gunman on a Los Angeles road. Within weeks of this personal tragedy, Cosby was on television and on the road, continuing to do what he does best, making people laugh.

Suggested Activities

Read, Watch, and Listen: Share excerpts from some of Cosby's books with your class. Also, watch a videotape of *The Cosby Show* and listen to one of his recordings. Most of Cosby's work is acceptable for people of all ages. Use your own discretion.

Writing: In small groups, write original scripts for episodes of *The Cosby Show*.

Meryl Streep

One of the most celebrated actresses of the eighties was Meryl Streep. Her performances in movies beginning in the seventies brought her to the public's attention, and an Academy Award in 1979 brought even greater notoriety. Throughout the eighties, she was universally considered to be among the greatest living actresses.

Mary Louise Streep was born in Summit, New Jersey, in 1949. She began voice lessons when she was twelve, which led to starring roles in several high school musicals. Streep became a student of acting at Vassar College, where she received her bachelor's degree, and continued her studies as part of the Vermont Repertory Company. Later she received her master's of fine arts at the Yale School of Drama, and she received an honorary degree from Dartmouth in 1981. Streep made her stage debut in New York City in 1975 with the New York Shakespeare Festival. She won critical acclaim for her performances in a variety of key roles, including *The Taming of the Shrew*.

Meryl Streep

Streep's movie debut in *Julia* in 1977 drew the attention of critics and audiences alike. Her first major role was in *The Deer Hunter* in 1978, and she was nominated for an Academy Award. She won an Emmy Award in 1978 for her role in television's *Holocaust*. This was followed by *Manhattan*, *The Seduction of Joe Tynan*, and *Kramer vs. Kramer* in 1979. Her role in *Kramer* earned her the 1979 Academy Award for Best Supporting Actress. In 1982, she won an Academy Award as Best Actress for her memorable performance in *Sophie's Choice*.

In *Sophie's Choice*, Streep demonstrated her ability to believably imitate a wide range of dialects and accents. In the film she spoke both English with a Polish accent and Polish. She has managed Italian, American midwestern, and other accents, all with seeming ease. The actress is also noted for the variety of characters she can play. There is no one "Meryl Streep"-type character. She plays them all.

Throughout the years, Streep has been nominated for and won a variety of acting awards, including the Emmy, Oscar, Golden Globe, National Society of Film Critics Award, Los Angeles Film Critics Award, New York Film Critics Award, Obie Award, and Cannes Film Festival Award. Her honors and acclaim indicate that she will be remembered as one of the best actresses ever.

Suggested Activities

Listen and Record: Listen to a recording of Streep's 1985 narration of *The Velveteen Rabbit*. Make recordings of your favorite children's books, using Streep's model as an example.

Acting: Work in groups to prepare one-act skits for the class. The class can vote on the skit they think was best presented.

Barbara Walters

Barbara Walters was a broadcast journalist long before the eighties, and by 1976, she was the first female co-anchor on a television news show and the highest-paid reporter in the world with a million-dollar-a-year salary. Her renowned interview specials also began in 1976, so her name and face were well established by 1980. That is exactly why she is included here: Barbara Walters was a staple of television throughout the decade.

Born Barbara Jill Walters in 1929, she moved up the ladder of broadcast journalism like no woman had before her. For her, pursuit of her career was relentless. She covered Kennedy's assassination and funeral, Fidel Castro considered her his favorite journalist, Ted Kennedy granted her an exclusive interview after the tragedy at Chappaquiddick, and Middle Eastern leaders Anwar el-Sadat and Menachem Begin provided her with an unheard-of joint interview.

Barbara Walters

Walters spent years working her way through the rank and file of network journalism. In the sixties, she was asked to host *Today* on NBC. It was a golden opportunity, and she held the position for fifteen years. She then became the first woman to co-anchor a nightly news show, also on NBC. In 1976, she moved to ABC, joining Harry Reasoner as co-anchor of the network's nightly news. Reasoner, however, did not want to share his anchor spot with Walters. She moved to another ABC show, *20/20*, a weekly news magazine, which she has co-anchored with Hugh Downs for more than two decades.

For all of her work and accomplishments, Barbara Walters is probably best known for her series featuring interviews with famous and infamous people. The programs began in the late seventies and are aired as specials by the network. On each, she interviews three famous people, usually from the fields of politics, entertainment, or sports. Some of her interviews have become classics in terms of television history. People still jokingly ask Walter's famous question, first asked of actress Katherine Hepburn: "If you were a tree, what kind would you be?" (Hepburn answered "An oak.")

Although it seems that Walters' professional star was always on the rise, her personal life was often troubled, sad, and lonely. She experienced a sad, although pampered, childhood, marred by the death of an older brother and her parents' great sadness over the retardation of her older sister. Walters herself said that she had trouble accepting and coping with her sister's handicap. The losses from Walter's childhood crept over into her adulthood. She has divorced three times and experienced prolonged estrangements and conflict with her only child, a daughter.

Suggested Activities

Interview: View a variety of Walter's interviews if you have access to them. Study the way she conducts her interviews. Discuss what you see, and then conduct your own interviews of one another. Carefully plan questions and practice their techniques. If successful, it would be worthwhile to let them interview individuals brought into the classroom (for example, local workers and career people).

Video: As a class, write a news program and videotape it like a nightly news show. If desired, small groups of students can prepare individual broadcasts.

Edward James Olmos

Edward James Olmos was the second child of Pedro Olmos, a Mexican immigrant, and Eleanor Huizar, a native of Los Angeles. Eddie, as he was called, was born on February 24, 1947, in East Los Angeles. When his parents divorced, Olmos and his sister visited their father on the weekends. Pedro loved dancing the mambo and the jitterbug. Eddie and his sister convinced their father to teach them the dances, and often the three would dance around the kitchen during their time together. Eddie knew that music and dance would always be a part of his life.

Olmos discovered musical performance when he was thirteen, and by the time he was a high school senior, he was in a rock band. When he graduated in 1964, he was already earning a living playing music. He formed a band called The Pacific Ocean, and it became very popular. The band played at such high-profile clubs as Gazzarri's and The Factory. While performing, Olmos also attended college. He studied psychology, criminology, dance, and theater. He worked diligently at his schoolwork, knowing that a good education was crucial for success.

While working at The Factory, Olmos met Kaija, a patron, and fell in love. The two were married a year later. Once married, he quit the band and began pursuing acting full time. He made a Spanish movie called *¡El Alambrista!* which won an award at the Cannes Film Festival in 1977. The next year, Olmos got the lead role in a play called *Zoot Suit*. To prepare for his role, he painstakingly researched all aspects of a Chicano group called the Zooters from the 1940s. Olmos earned rave reviews for his performance, including a nomination for the Tony Award and the Los Angeles Drama Critics Circle Award for Best Actor. When the play moved to New York, Olmos traveled with it, fulfilling a lifelong dream. There he made a vow to take only roles that inspired people. Although Olmos was actively pursued by Hollywood, all the roles depicted criminals and corrupt individuals. He refused them all, turning down great sums of money in the process.

In 1982, the role he had been waiting for came along when the Public Broadcasting System offered him the part of a Mexican cowhand named Gregorio Cortez, a character of virtue and integrity. Olmos again painstakingly researched the part. He also wrote all the music for the movie. The next big break came in 1984 when he was offered the role of Lieutenant Martin Castillo in a new television series called *Miami Vice*. The show became one of the most popular of the eighties, and in 1985, Olmos won an Emmy for the role. In 1988, he accepted the role of Jaime Escalante, a real-life teacher who dramatically influenced the lives of students. This was another role of which Olmos could be proud. He researched the role by actually spending time with and observing Escalante. Olmos received an Oscar nomination for his performance in this film (*Stand and Deliver*).

In 1992, Olmos released a film close to his heart, entitled *American Me*. It was intended to show the vicious cycle of poverty, ignorance, and prejudice that held back his fellow Chicanos. That year, Olmos also made headlines by leading clean-up brigades through the streets of riot-torn Los Angeles.

Olmos continues to make films and pursue projects that will inspire people.

Suggested Activity

Acting: Chose an individual whose life inspires you. Write a short monlogue that will present that person to the class. Perform the skits.

Pop Culture

If you were a child of the eighties, most or all of the items on this page would have meaning for you. They were all part of popular culture during the ninth decade of the twentieth century. You can use this page in a variety of ways.

- Read the list to determine how many of the items you can identify.

- Interview someone who was old enough to be culturally aware in the eighties, and ask him or her to identify as many items on the list as possible.

- Use the items to create a 1980s trivia game. (See page 70.)

- Write a story that takes place in the 1980s. Incorporate as many items as possible from the list into your story.

You know you were a child of the eighties if you can remember . . .

- Scooby Doo
- Atari 2600
- Frogger
- E.T.
- G.I. Joe
- Malibu Barbie
- Rubik's Cube
- Dungeons & Dragons
- The Breakfast Club
- School House Rock
- Space Ghost
- *Indiana Jones*
- muppets
- Trivial Pursuit
- *M*A*S*H*

- *Cheers*
- PeeWee Herman
- The Bangles
- *Ghostbusters*
- "Beat It"
- Mr. T
- *The Cosby Show*
- *Knight Rider*
- *Fame*
- *Flashdance*
- *Dynasty*
- friendship bracelets
- New Coke
- Scategories
- *Born in the U.S.A.*

- "Little Pink Houses"
- The Material Girl
- Debbie Gibson
- Tiffany
- Boy George
- The Original MTV VJs
- *St. Elmo's Fire*
- Garbage Pail Kids
- Cabbage Patch Kids
- My Little Pony
- He-man and She-ra
- William "Refrigerator" Perry

- Underoos
- Jellies and Jams
- Jordache
- Guess
- Max Headroom
- Beta recording
- Alf
- Alex P. Keaton
- "Where's the beef?"
- slouch socks
- shoulder pads
- Teddy Ruxpin
- Mary Lou Retton

Trivial Matters

One of the hottest crazes of the eighties and among the most popular games in history, Trivial Pursuit® was the brainchild of photo editor Chris Haney and sportswriter Scott Abbott. They created the game in December 1979 while playing another popular game, Scrabble®.

The five Ws and current events were to be the backbone of their game. They called it Trivia Pursuit, until Haney's wife suggested the name that would stick, Trivial Pursuit.

The game they conceived consisted of trivia questions in six color-coded categories: geography (blue), entertainment (pink), art & literature (brown), history (yellow), science & nature (green), and sports & leisure (orange). Players would answer questions corresponding to the color on the playing board on which they had landed. At certain designated spaces, they could earn a piece of the pie, which was the game playing marker. After collecting all six pieces, the player makes his or her way to the center of the board for a final question and a win.

To produce their game, the men formed a company, bringing John Haney (Chris' brother) and his friend Ed Werner on board. Next came the need for funding, and this they got primarily from investors. The original thirty-four investors were, by and large, people the men knew, including a copyboy from the newspaper where they worked. In total, they took in $40,000. They proceeded to rent an office. To pay for help, they offered shares in the company.

The first 1,100 games cost approximately $75 each to produce, but they sold them to dealers for just $15 each. It was hardly a sound business approach; therefore, the company had acquired significant debt by 1982. However, at this time the game company Selchow and Righter became aware of their product and was interested. Selchow and Righter hired a public relations professional to market the game. The P.R. consultant oversaw a direct mail campaign to nearly 2,000 buyers at the 1983 New York Toy Fair. That was the beginning of history.

News of the game spread quickly through word of mouth. By the end of 1983, three-and-one-half million games had been sold. That figure skyrocketed to twenty million in 1984. By the end of the nineties, the still popular game had amassed retail sales over $1 billion.

Trivial Pursuit is produced today in nineteen languages and in a variety of versions in addition to the original Genus version. Other versions include Sports; Baby Boomers; Music; Eighties; Young Players; Genus II, III, and IV; and more. There is truly something for everyone with a mind for trivia.

In the following years, countless copycat games capitalized on the game's success, but the original Trivial Pursuit is by far the most well known and biggest seller.

Suggested Activities

Challenge: In small groups, write trivia questions in the same categories as the game. Exchange questions with another group for them to answer. Which group is able to answer the most questions correctly?

Eighties: Create a Trivial Pursuit bulletin board with trivia questions and answers related directly to the eighties. Make it a class project to find and post the trivia. Divide the board into categories of your choice, or use the same ones on the original Trivial Pursuit game.

The Look of the Times

The eighties had a style all their own. Women in the work force began to wear power suits just like the men. Some even accessorized with neckties. Formally, the *Dynasty* look of designer gowns, jewels, and big hair was popular. Casually, women wore plenty of leggings, designer jeans, polo shirts, western clothing, penny loafers, padded shoulders, stonewashed jeans, and skirts ranging from mini to "tea" length. Makeup was generally heavy with dark browns and mauves. Hair was big, big, big or ultra short and coifed. Headbands and athletic wear were everyday attire.

Here and on the next page are some typical outfits from the era. Use them to study or to color.

Challenge: Design other clothing in typical 1980's styles.

The Look of the Times *(cont.)*

Men had a unique style in the eighties. Power suits were part of the necessary equipment for the business man. Casually, men wore slacks with printed shirts, polo shirts and long cotton shorts, sockless loafers, and the *Miami Vice* look of casual, light-colored suits over darker T-shirts. Sunglasses and five o'clock shadows completed the look. New Wave and other musical movements had their effects, and a variety of wild hairstyles, animal prints, and even feminine makeup became part of men's attire.

Elsewhere

This chronology gives a few of the important events around the globe during the 1980s. Have students research further any people and events that interest them.

1980

- Robert Mugabe is elected prime minister of Zimbabwe.
- Andre Sakharov, Nobel physicist, is sent into exile in Gorky in the USSR.
- A bomb planted in Bologna, Italy, kills 84 and injures more than 200.
- The Olympic Games in Moscow are boycotted by several countries, including the US, due to the Soviet occupation in Afghanistan.

1981

- There is civil war in Lebanon.
- Solidarity's first national conference is held in Poland.

1982

- Argentina and the UK go to war in the Falkland Islands.
- Israel returns Sinai to Egypt in accordance with the Camp David agreement.
- Italy's forty-third government since 1945 takes control.

1983

- The USSR joins the U.S. in Strategic Arms Reduction Talks.
- Benigno Aquino, Philippine presidential hopeful, is assassinated at the Manila Airport.
- A South Korean plane is shot down over the USSR, killing all 269 passengers.

1984

- The US pilot shot down over Lebanon is released by Syria after Jesse Jackson intervenes.
- British coal miners strike through the year.
- Indian Prime Minister Indira Gandhi is assassinated.
- The USSR and other nations boycott the Olympics in Los Angeles in retaliation for the 1980 boycott.

1985

- Daniel Ortega becomes the president of Nicaragua.
- Mikhail Gorbachev becomes the new General Secretary of the USSR.
- US sanctions are made against South Africa in protest of apartheid.

1986

- Corazón Aquino becomes the president of the Philippines. Ferdinand Marcos and his wife flee the country.
- The European Community adopts sanctions against South Africa. President Botha announces a national state of emergency.

1987

- Terry Waite, the Archbishop of Canterbury's envoy, is kidnapped in Lebanon while seeking the release of Western hostages.
- Margaret Thatcher is elected Prime Minister of the UK for the third time.
- Gorbachev and Reagan sign a treaty banning all short- and medium-range nuclear weapons in Europe.

1988

- Benazir Bhutto is named Prime Minister of Pakistan.
- Soviet troops begin to withdraw from Afghanistan.
- Iran and Iraq begin peace talks, accepting a UN peace plan.

1989

- Martial law in China puts an end to student demonstrations for democracy in Tiananmen Square, Peking.
- Solidarity is victorious in the Polish parliamentary elections.
- The Berlin Wall comes down.

Passages

Births

1980

- Chelsea Clinton, only child of American President Bill Clinton
- MaCauley Culkin, American actor

1981

- Jonathan Taylor Thomas, American actor

1982

- Prince William Arthur Philip Louis, heir apparent to the British throne
- Dominique Moceanu, US Olympic gymnast
- LeAnn Rimes, American country music singer

1984

- "Baby Fae," infant born with defective heart; receives transplant of heart from baboon

- Prince Henry Charles Alfred David Windsor, younger son of Prince Charles and Princess Diana

1985

- Alexandra Nechita, professional artist (sold $2 million of her art by age eleven)

1987

- South African triplets, carried and delivered by their mother's mother
- Yugoslavian boy, the five billionth inhabitant of the world (according to the UN Secretary General)

1989

- Jessica Dubroff, died in 1996 while attempting to be the youngest pilot ever to cross the US

Deaths

1980

- Mae West, American actress
- Jean-Paul Sartre, French philosopher and author
- Henry Miller, American author
- Marshall McLuhan, Canadian media author
- Jimmy Durante, American comedian
- Sir Alfred Hitchcock, English-born, American movie director
- John Lennon, English musician
- Jean Piaget, Swiss psychologist
- Colonel Harland Sanders, American restaurateur
- Jesse Owens, American athlete

1981

- Christy Brown, Irish novelist and artist
- Hoagy Carmichael, American songwriter
- Bill Haley, American rock star
- Joe Louis, American boxing champion
- Anwar el-Sadat, Egyptian president
- Natalie Wood, American actress
- Bob Marley, Jamaican musician

1982

- John Cheever, American writer
- Ayn Rand, American novelist
- Satchel Paige, American baseball player
- Menachem Begin, Israel's prime minister
- Henry Fonda and John Belushi, American actors
- Grace Kelly, princess of Monaco and former American actress

1983

- Benigno Aquino, Philippine presidential hopeful
- Umberto, last King of Italy
- Tennessee Williams, American playwright
- Buckminster Fuller, American philosopher and architect
- Karen Carpenter, American singer
- Ira Gershwin, American lyricist
- Muddy Waters, American blues musician

1984

- Truman Capote, American writer
- Ansel Adams, American photographer
- Marvin Gaye, American singer
- Ethel Merman, American singer
- Ray Kroc, founder of McDonald's

1985

- Orson Welles, American filmmaker
- Laura Ashley, English designer
- Yul Brynner, American actor
- Marc Chagall, Russian artist
- Rock Hudson, American actor
- Dian Fossey, American zoologist

1986

- Olaf Palme, Swedish prime minister
- James Cagney and Cary Grant, American actors
- Georgia O'Keefe, American artist
- Benny Goodman, American bandleader

1987

- Andy Warhol, American artist
- James Baldwin, American novelist
- Fred Astaire and Danny Kaye, American actors and dancers
- Maria von Trapp, Austrian singer and author
- Andres Segovia, Spanish classical guitarist

1988

- Sean MacBride, Irish politician and Nobel Peace Prize winner
- Robert Heinlein, American writer of science fiction
- Roy Orbison, American singer

1989

- Hirohito, Emperor of Japan
- Samuel Beckett, Irish author
- Sir Laurence Olivier, English actor
- Lucille Ball and Bette Davis, American actresses
- Salvador Dali, Spanish artist
- Irving Berlin, American songwriter
- Sugar Ray Robinson, American boxer
- Nicolae Ceausescu, Romania's president

Terrorism

It seemed throughout the 1980s that acts of terrorism around the world were an almost constant occurrence. Travelers and citizens around the globe reacted in fear and trepidation. Here are a few of the significant terrorist events.

TWA Flight 847 On June 14, 1985, TWA Flight 847, bound for Rome, Italy, from Athens, Greece, was hijacked just after takeoff by two armed men. There were 153 passengers on board. The gunmen, members of the Islamic Jihad ("holy war") forced the plane to fly to Beirut, Lebanon, and to land there. In Beirut, the hijackers demanded that Israel release 766 prisoners, primarily Shiite Muslims. Members of the Shiite militia joined the hijackers on the plane, and together they had the plane fly back and forth between Beirut and Algiers four times. Between each flight, some hostages were freed and one, an American, was killed. The remaining thirty-nine American male passengers were held captive in Beirut. At first, the United States and Israel held strong against the terrorist tactics, but on June 24, Israel released 31 prisoners, although they said that the release was unconnected with the hostage situation. On June 30, the remaining hostages were freed.

Achille Lauro On October 7, 1985, an Italian cruise ship called the *Achille Lauro* sailed off the coast of Egypt. Four gunmen seized the ship, which held 400 passengers. The men were members of the Palestine Liberation Front (PLF), a guerilla faction of the Palestine Liberation Organization (PLO). They threatened to blow up the ship unless Israel agreed to release fifty PLO prisoners. To demonstrate that they meant what they said, the terrorists killed one passenger, Leon Klinghoffer, a 69-year-old Jewish-American man who was confined to a wheelchair. His body was thrown overboard. On October 9, Egypt's president Hosti Mubarak and PLF leader Mohammed Abbas persuaded the terrorists to give up. The United States demanded that they be charged and punished. Instead, Mubarak released the terrorists to Abbas, and the group boarded a commercial Egyptian flight bound for Tunisia. On the next day, U.S. jets intercepted the Egyptian plane and forced it to land in Sicily, where the terrorists were turned over to the Italian government.

Pan Am Flight 103 On December 21, 1988, Pan Am Flight 103 exploded in midair over Lockerbie, Scotland. All 259 passengers and crew members were killed. Eleven people on the ground were also killed, and two rows of houses were destroyed. Investigators looked for a cause for the crash of the plane, which simply disappeared from radar screens while flying from London to New York. British investigators discovered that the plane had been blown apart by a bomb hidden in a suitcase stored in the luggage compartment of the plane. Terrorists had planted the bomb, and evidence eventually led to two Libyans. However, they were protected by their government, which would not release them for trial.

Suggested Activities

Research: Find out more about the Islamic Jihad and PLO. Learn why terrorist actions are sometimes a part of their activities.

History: Learn about the role of terrorism throughout history, from ancient times to the present.

Anwar el-Sadat

In 1918, Anwar el-Sadat was born in Egypt near the Nile River Delta. After his graduation from the Egyptian Military Academy in 1938, he joined with Gamal Abdel Nasser and other militants to overthrow British rule in Egypt. He served time in prison for his revolutionary activities, but in 1952, he and the others were successful in overthrowing King Faruk. Sadat quickly rose through the ranks of Egypt's government after that, serving as vice president from 1954 to 1967 and again from 1969 to 1970 under the presidency of Nasser.

When Nasser died, Sadat became president and remained the leader until his death. Sadat continued the work of Nasser, calling for the return of the Sinai Peninsula and Gaza Strip from Israelis, who had held the land since 1967. Disputes over Gaza and conflict between the two nations date to ancient times.

Anwar el-Sadat

Sadat became world renowned for his peacemaking efforts with Israel. In 1977, Sadat met with Israel's leader, Menachem Begin, and offered recognition of Israel on certain conditions. In 1978, American President Jimmy Carter arranged meetings with the two leaders at Camp David to end the Arab-Israeli conflict. They reached an agreement that included a peace treaty between the two nations and the withdrawal of Israel from the Sinai. It also called for self-government for the Gaza Strip. The treaty was officially signed in 1979, and Israel completely left the Sinai in 1982. Sadat and Begin shared the Nobel Peace Prize in 1978 for their work.

Although nations around the world applauded the work of Sadat, many in his own country were angry. Other Arab leaders felt that he had acted independently, and they were unhappy with his work. On October 6, 1981, Anwar el-Sadat was assassinated in the city of Cairo by a group of religious militants from his own country. Their reason for the assassination was opposition to Sadat's policies.

Suggested Activities

Leaders: Learn about Menachem Begin and his contributions to Israel. Also learn about Jimmy Carter's role in the negotiations and what his motives were.

Cartography: Draw maps of Egypt and Israel, pinpointing the sources of conflict between the two nations in the late seventies.

Today: Research to find out about the relationship between Egypt and Israel today. What strides have been taken, both forward and backward?

Middle East: Throughout the eighties, there was a great deal of conflict in many areas of the Middle East. Other topics and places to research and to learn about include Iraq and Iran, the *USS Stark*, Lebanese Civil War, Shiites, and the Palestine Liberation Organization (PLO).

Marathon of Hope

Cancer is a disease that causes aberrations in normal body cells and tumorous growths. One young Canadian, Terry Fox, fought valiantly in 1980 to end the suffering caused by cancer.

Terrence Stanley Fox was born in Winnipeg, Manitoba, Canada, in 1958 and grew up in British Columbia. In 1977, while still a teenager, Fox was diagnosed with bone cancer. Due to this illness, his doctors thought it best to amputate his right leg above the knee. From that time forward, Fox used an artificial leg, learning to walk and even to run.

While receiving treatment for cancer, Fox developed empathy for the suffering he saw around him in the hospitals and treatment centers. He knew firsthand that cancer was a painful disease. He felt inspired to make a difference, so he began to run.

Fox trained for more than a year, conditioning himself as a marathon runner. Then, in April 1980, at St. John's, Newfoundland, Fox began what he called the Marathon of Hope. In this marathon, Fox intended to run across the entire width of Canada, raising money for cancer research while he ran. He called his run a marathon because he intended to run a marathon length, 26 miles (42 kilometers), each day.

In all, Fox ran for a total of 143 days, each day averaging his desired distance. He ran through all sorts of weather conditions, including hail, snow, and grueling heat. His total distance was 3,339 miles (5,374 kilometers); however, this distance was short of his desired goal. On September 1, 1980, Fox was forced to stop near Thunder Bay, Ontario. His cancer had spread to his lungs. He was hospitalized for treatment and died ten months later without returning to his marathon. However, during the time he did run, he earned twenty-five million dollars for cancer research.

Before his death, Fox was awarded Canada's highest honor for civilians, the Order of Canada. Since the time of his death, marathons have been run annually in Fox's memory. These annual runs also raise money for cancer research.

In 1985, another cancer amputee, Steve Fonyo, ran the entire distance that Terry Fox had intended to run. Nineteen-year-old Fonyo ran a total of 4,924 miles (7,920 kilometers) across the nation of Canada. The run took him a total of fourteen months.

Suggested Activities

Research: Find out about the disease of cancer and the advances that have been made in its treatment since 1980.

Special Athletes: There are a number of athletes who play and compete with physical and mental challenges. Learn about one or some of these athletes and the odds they overcame to play their sport.

Marathons: The marathon originated in ancient Greece. Learn about its history.

Cartography: Draw a map of Canada, marking the distance across the nation at quarterly intervals. Draw a line showing Terry Fox's path from Newfoundland to Thunder Bay, Ontario.

Corazón Aquino

Corazón Aquino

From 1965 until 1986, the Philippines were led by President Ferdinand Marcos. A World War II hero, Marcos was a popular leader until he established martial law in the early seventies and gave himself even more power. Under his leadership, the country grew increasingly impoverished. In 1981, Marcos lifted martial law and returned law-making rights to the National Assembly. He even released some political prisoners. The president was re-elected for another six years.

At this time, another leader, Benigno Aquino, was gaining in popularity. Aquino was a leading member of the opposition party when martial law was declared in 1972. He was imprisoned from 1972 until 1980, when he was allowed to move his family to the United States. In August of 1983, he returned to the Philippines to work in the legislative election. In spite of high security, he was killed by an unknown gunman when he disembarked from his plane in Manila.

Marcos denied having anything to do with the assassination, and the gunman could not be linked to any political faction. However, the people did not believe Marcos, and many began to riot and protest. They called for Marcos' resignation.

Corazón Aquino returned to the Philippines for her husband's funeral and stayed to work in the legislative election campaign. The opposition party won one third of the seats in 1984. When Marcos called for a presidential election in 1986, Corazón Aquino became the opposition candidate. The people rallied behind her. Marcos declared himself the winner of the February 7 election and staged his inauguration on February 25. Popular demonstrations and an army revolt led to the inauguration of Aquino on the same day. Faced with charges of murder and election fraud, Marcos and his wife fled the country by helicopter, seeking asylum in the United States. Aquino formed a provisional government, and many nations around the world recognized her as the new leader. She was the first female leader of the Philippine nation.

The situation in the Philippines did not improve dramatically with the removal of Marcos, but the people did rally behind Aquino. She implemented a new constitution and held a legislative election in 1987. Poverty and a poor economy were still of great concern. Communist insurgents carried on with political assassinations and guerilla activity. In 1989, rebels in the Philippine military attempted to take over the government. However, the United States, under the leadership of President George Bush, stepped in to aid Aquino and the Philippine government. The rebels were quickly overthrown.

By the close of the decade, Aquino was still in power, but her troubles were not over. Turmoil in the Philippines continued, although many believed that the government under her leadership was far superior to that of the previous two decades. Slowly, the economy did begin to grow, but Aquino chose to leave office in 1992, declining to run for another term.

Suggested Activities

Women: Aquino is one of several women who came to or experienced political prominence throughout the world in the eighties. Find out about another such woman and write her story.

Cartography: Draw a map of the Philippines.

Colors: Aquino consistently wore yellow throughout the election and the beginning of her presidency. Find out the reason for her color choice.

Indira Gandhi

Indira Gandhi was the first female prime minister in India, elected in 1966. Born to an influential family in Allahabad, India, she held the office of prime minister from 1966 to 1977 and again from 1980 until her assassination in 1984.

Indira Gandhi

Born November 19, 1917, Indira Priyadarshini Nehru was the daughter and only child of Jawaharlal Nehru. From childhood, the country's politics played a great part in her life. Her grandfather was a leader in India's fight for independence from Britain, and her father was India's first prime minister from 1947 to 1964. She graduated from Visva-Bharati University in Bengal and studied at Oxford University in England. In 1942, she married a lawyer, Feroze Gandhi (no relation to the Indian freedom leader, Mohandas Gandhi). Shortly after their marriage, the couple spent thirteen months in prison for their part in India's Independence Party, which sought freedom from Britain. Feroze Gandhi died in 1960.

When India became independent and Gandhi's father took office as prime minister, she served as his official hostess and as one of his advisors. She also accompanied him on trips. In 1955, Gandhi was elected to the executive body of the Indian National Congress party and in 1959, became its president.

After her father's death in 1964, Gandhi became India's minister of information and broadcasting under Prime Minister Lal Bahadur Shastri. When Shastri died in 1966, Indira Gandhi succeeded him. The following year she was elected to the office of prime minister by the Congress party. In 1971, she led her party to a landslide victory.

In June of 1975, a court found Gandhi guilty of illegal campaign practices during the 1971 election. Many called for her resignation. Gandhi responded by declaring a state of emergency two weeks after the ruling, arresting many of her opponents and censoring the press. In 1977, she called for a new election, which she hoped would demonstrate popular support for her regime. The Congress party suffered a sweeping defeat, and she was voted out of office. However, she made a comeback in the elections held in January of 1980 and formed a new majority government.

In 1984, Gandhi moved to suppress Sikh insurgents. The capture of the Golden Temple in Amritsar, the headquarters of the Sikh religious faction, outraged many of the group's members. On October 31, 1984, two Sikh members of her security guard shot her at very close range, killing her.

Suggested Activities

Assassination: Many world leaders of the twentieth century were assassinated. Learn who they were and why they were assassinated. Also find out about failed assassination attempts.

Politics: In the twentieth century, the political climate in India has changed dramatically, largely due to the freedom the nation gained from Britain in the 1940s. Find out about India's political history over the last century.

Mikhail Gorbachev

Mikhail Sergei Gorbachev was born in Privolnoye, Russia, on March 2, 1931, to peasant farmers. In 1952, while attending the university in Moscow, he joined the Communist Party. After receiving a law degree in 1955, Gorbachev pursued a career with the Communist Party. He worked his way up, becoming the head of the regional Communist Party Committee in 1970. In 1980, he became a full member of the Communist Party's chief policymaking division, called the *Politburo*.

Mikhail Gorbachev

At this time, the general secretary of the Communist Party was the ranking Soviet leader and the most powerful political figure. When Yuri Andropov became secretary general in 1982, he placed Gorbachev at the helm of the nation's economic policy. Andropov died in 1984 and was replaced by Konstantin U. Chernenko. When Chernenko died in 1985, Gorbachev became the general secretary (head) of the Communist Party. In 1988, he assumed the title of chairman of the Presidium of the Supreme Soviet, or president of the U.S.S.R., a post that was largely ceremonial but which under his leadership gained in significance.

The youngest Soviet leader since Stalin, Gorbachev differed from previous Soviet leaders in other ways as well. Most Soviet leaders had not been college-educated; and unlike his predecessors, who usually stayed within Soviet borders, Gorbachev traveled the world.

Gorbachev is best remembered for the work he did from 1985 through 1991 as the last leader of the Soviet Union. He initiated *perestroika* (reform), a program of economic and political reform, and encouraged *glasnost* (openness) in political and cultural affairs. In 1990, Gorbachev won the Nobel Peace Prize for his painstaking work toward world peace and the strides he made in Soviet relations with nations around the world.

Many other nations looked on with approval at the changes Gorbachev brought to the Soviet Union, but those changes were instrumental in bringing the end of the U.S.S.R. in 1991.

Gorbachev worked diligently to keep the Soviet Union together while bringing about his reforms. In 1991, he resigned as Communist party general secretary, appointed reformers to head the military and KGB, and permitted Estonia, Latvia, and Lithuania to become independent republics. On December 8, 1991, the U.S.S.R. voted itself out of existence, and on December 25 of the same year, Gorbachev resigned as president.

Gorbachev continued to work in politics after his resignation, primarily with the Foundation for Social, Economic, and Political Research, sometimes called the Gorbachev Foundation, in Moscow.

Suggested Activities

Communism: Research to find out what communism is, how it started, and where it exists in the world today.

History: Learn about the formation of the Soviet Union as well as its destruction. Also learn about the significant players in the beginning and in the end.

Tiananmen Square Massacre

Following the death of former Communist Party Secretary General of China Hu Yaobang in April of 1989, students began peaceful memorial demonstrations in several cities. They considered Hu a hero because he had favored liberalization and modernization. Pro-democracy demonstrations continued and grew as participants ignored the government's demand that they end their actions.

In May of 1989, Soviet president Mikhail Gorbachev traveled to China to discuss improving relations between the Soviets and China. Approximately two million people, primarily Chinese students, gathered in the streets to support Gorbachev and his policy of *glasnost* (openness) in the Soviet Union. Several thousand more students gathered in Tiananmen Square in Beijing, staging a hunger strike to protest their government and as a call for democracy. The Chinese government, embarrassed by the actions of the young people, kept Gorbachev away from the square.

Martial law was declared on May 20; however, other protestors around the nation began to rally as well. Chinese troops were sent to stop the protestors, but the people blocked their passage. Some even lay down in the streets. In the end, however, the protestors proved no match for the government troops. At first many protestors were arrested, including some who built a model of America's Statue of Liberty in the capital city's square. Then the troops moved to stop the protests completely. Tanks began to roll, driving over everyone and everything that stood in their way. Thousands of guns were fired, and many people were killed in one of the most brutal massacres in history. It was reported by the protest leaders that approximately two to five thousand people were killed by the troops, although the exact number may never be known. International television cameras and journalists captured much of the violence. Later, the government banned the foreign press and conducted widespread arrests, summary trials, and executions. The government refused to make public the names of those who died.

Deng Xiaoping called the protesters thugs and hoodlums. He went on Chinese television to declare that their insurgency against the government had been squelched and that their threat to the national welfare was ended.

Many nations protested the actions of the government. Chinese relations with some Western nations, including the United States, took a turn for the worse. Making matters worse, the Chinese government officially stated that the massacre at Tiananmen Square had never happened. Even in the face of witnesses and cameras, they declared this to be true. The government had tried to rewrite history; however, modern communication made this impossible.

Suggested Activities

Politics: Learn about the politics of China today, as well as the feelings of any dissenting groups.

Protests: In the United States in the sixties and seventies, a number of student groups held protests for a variety of reasons. They met with different kinds of opposition and different results. Learn about some of them and the effects of their protests.

Cartography: Draw maps of modern China; include the capital city of Beijing.

Polish Solidarity

Government in Poland changed dramatically in the 1980s. That was due in large part to a group called Solidarity and to a man named Lech Walesa.

Walesa was a shipyard worker in Poland in 1980. At that time, workers decided to strike to protest poor working conditions and low wages. Workers first staged a strike at a shipyard in Gdansk. The strike spread, and soon workers from other yards and factories were striking. In all, half a million workers took part in the strikes. The striking workers called for the release of political prisoners, improved labor laws, and the right to free speech. They continued their strike for two months, and it finally proved successful. Lech Walesa emerged as the leader of the strikes and of Solidarity.

The government gave in to the striking workers and allowed them to form a trade union. This was the first time that a communist nation supported the development of a union.

Lech Walesa

Workers in various places around Poland continued to hold strikes and to make other demands. When the government changed hands in 1981, the new leader, General Wojciech Jaruzelski, wanted to put an end to the workers' protests. Jaruzelski increased the military's power, banned public meetings and demonstrations, and outlawed Solidarity. Lech Walesa and other workers were arrested.

On May 1, 1982, Labor Day in many nations around the world, thousands of workers marched through Warsaw, protesting the government's military rule and calling for the support of Solidarity. Their protests served to heighten government control. The Polish government canceled major sporting events and banned the use of private automobiles.

The actions of Jaruzelski had international effects. Some nations, such as the Soviet Union, supported him; others, like the United States, spoke out in protest. President Ronald Reagan revoked the "most-favored nation" status that Poland enjoyed with the United States. This status had kept export charges from Poland to the United States low. The revocation hurt Poland economically.

Once again, the government was forced to relent. Walesa and others were released from prison, and in 1983, Walesa received the Nobel Peace Prize for his efforts to bring reform and peace to Poland.

Tensions and protests continued throughout the following years. In 1988, strikes became rampant throughout Poland. The government was forced to meet with Solidarity leaders, including Walesa, to discuss negotiations. In 1989, the government officially recognized Solidarity as a legal union. The union then became a political party, and many of its leaders were elected to the Polish National Assembly. Lech Walesa himself was elected as president in 1990. Solidarity had succeeded in overthrowing the communist government.

Suggested Activities

Politics: Learn about the politics and government of Poland today, as well as prior to the communist takeover.

Cartography: Draw maps of Poland; include the capital city of Warsaw.

Charles and Diana

The royal romance that opened the decade grew to be a royal failure by the next, but in the beginning there was pageantry and fairy tale dreams come true.

Prince and Princess of Wales

The story began with His Royal Highness Charles Philip Arthur George, Prince of Wales, Duke of Cornwall, Earl of Chester, Duke of Rothesay, Earl of Carrick, Baron Renfrew, Lord of the Isles, Prince and Great Steward of Scotland—also known as Prince Charles. He asked Lady Diana Spencer, a British aristocrat, to be his bride. In all likelihood, she would one day become the queen of England just as Charles, as heir apparent, would be king. Nineteen-year-old Lady Diana accepted the proposal. In the following months, the media began to follow Lady Diana wherever she went. Soon, her popularity eclipsed that of the prince. Reporters found out everything about her life and history, and she was followed everywhere. Not only was she of interest as the future princess and, perhaps, queen, but also she was beautiful, charming, and engagingly shy with the camera. The public adored her.

On July 29, 1981, the couple were married. It is estimated that 700 million people watched the ceremony, which was aired on international television. As they watched, they saw the pomp and pageantry for which England is legendary. It seemed truly the stuff of which fairy tales are made.

The couple soon had two children, Prince William Arthur Philip Louis (next in line to his father for the throne) in 1982 and Prince Henry Charles Albert David in 1984. However, as time wore on, the media began to report that the couple's marriage was strained. News of their troubles and tensions began to appear in the papers almost daily. Although the palace denied the reports or refused to comment, the media coverage continued. Finally, amid great controversy, the couple separated in December of 1992 and later divorced. The controversy and scandal caused by the failed marriage, as well as the reasons for its failure, have caused a great deal of discussion concerning the future of the British monarchy. When Charles and Diana were married, it was widely rumored that Charles' mother, Queen Elizabeth, would abdicate the throne and allow her son to become king. However, a decade later, many began to suspect that Charles never would be king. The divorce settlement itself guaranteed that Diana would never be queen.

Tragically, on August 30, 1997, Diana and two others were killed in a car accident in France. International demonstrations of mourning were abundant.

Suggested Activities

Monarchy: Trace the line of the British monarchy; learn about some of the prominent and influential British monarchs over time. Also learn about the other existing monarchies of the world.

Fairy Tales: Another great romance in the 20th century history of the British monarchy is the story of King Edward and Wallis Simpson. Learn about the couple and what happened to them.

Today: Find out about Charles and his sons today as well as the state of the monarchy in England.

Pope John Paul II

Pope John Paul II, leader of the Roman Catholic Church, became one of the most influential leaders of the 1980s. He was also brought into the forefront due to a nearly successful assassination attempt on his life.

Pope John Paul II

He was born Karol Jozef Wojtyla in Wadowice, Poland, in 1920. During World War II, he worked in a stone quarry and a chemical factory while preparing for the priesthood at an underground seminary. After he was ordained a priest in 1946, he taught philosophy and ethics while serving as a chaplain for university students. He was appointed auxiliary bishop of Krakow in 1958, archbishop of Krakow in 1964, and he became a cardinal in 1967. In 1978, he was elected pope, the first non-Italian pope since Adrian VI of Holland in 1523.

In May of 1981, a Turkish terrorist named Mehmet Ali Agca shot Pope John Paul II as he entered Saint Peter's Square. The pope was severely wounded but recovered fully. He earned the admiration of many around the world when he went to his imprisoned attacker and forgave him for his actions. A second attempt was made on the pope's life during a 1982 visit to Portugal, but he was not injured. Since then the pope has taken great care in his audiences. Normally, he goes among the crowd in a specially designed vehicle with a large dome of bulletproof glass—"the pope-mobile" as it is affectionately referred to.

John Paul has published poetry and, under the name Andrzej Jawien, a play called *The Jeweler's Apprentice*. In addition, he has written several books on ethics and theology. Since becoming pope, he has published more than twelve encyclicals (letters) which address a variety of moral and theological issues.

John Paul's views are not always greeted with support. He tends to be conservative, sticking closely to traditional church views. At the same time, many in the Catholic Church differ with him on various topics, particularly the right of priests to marry and the right of women to become priests. John Paul adamantly opposes both. Also, he is a great proponent for world peace and international relations; his avowed goal is the unification of people. Many believe that due to his engaging and charismatic personality, he will go a long way in achieving his goal.

Throughout the eighties and nineties, John Paul traveled to Asia, Africa, and the Americas, visiting more than sixty nations and working to unite people around the world. He is credited with influencing the restoration of democracy and religious freedom in the countries of Eastern Europe, especially in Poland, his native land. In the nineties, he visited the Baltic republics, formerly members of the USSR. His meetings with world leaders from many nations were generally well received and successful.

Suggested Activities

Discussion: Discuss ways in which the people of the world might be brought closer together.

History: Learn about the history of the Roman Catholic Church as well as of the papacy.

The Iron Lady

Great Britain's government had a woman at the helm throughout the entire decade of the 1980s. Her name was Margaret Thatcher, but her country knew her as the Iron Lady.

Margaret Hilda Roberts was born in Grantham, Lincolnshire, England, in 1925. She attended Oxford University where she earned a degree in chemistry. In 1951, she married a businessman named Denis Thatcher, who was supportive of her education and political ambitions. She became a tax attorney in 1953.

Thatcher's political career began in 1959 when she was elected to Britain's House of Commons as a member of the Conservative Party. From 1970 to 1974, she served as secretary of state for education and science. The Conservative Party was defeated by the Labor Party in 1974. In 1975, Thatcher was elected to lead the Conservative Party, the first woman ever to hold that position.

In the last half of the seventies, times became difficult in Great Britain. The economy declined and there were numerous labor disputes. A labor strike kept oil from being delivered to homes, schools, and businesses during an especially cold winter. Thatcher attacked the Labor Party government and called on citizens to enter a vote of no confidence. In the election of 1979 they did so, electing Thatcher and her party. Margaret Thatcher became the first female prime minister of Great Britain.

Thatcher was a hard-line politician who stuck fiercely to her principles and beliefs. This is why she became known as the Iron Lady. She advocated a free-enterprise economy; tight monetary policies to control inflation, lower taxes, and lower government spending; privatization of nationalized industries (including health care, public housing, and schools); and restrictions on trade unions. Her policies, especially her emphasis on private enterprise, became known as "Thatcherism."

In 1982, Argentine forces occupied the Falkland Islands, which both Great Britain and Argentina claimed. Thatcher and her government sent a task force that defeated the Argentines. The success of the Falkland Islands policy aided in Thatcher's reelection in 1983.

In the years that followed, she met frequently with U.S. presidents Ronald Reagan and George Bush, strengthening Britain's Western alliance. She also called on Mikhail Gorbachev and established a working relationship. Thatcher was recognized as a world leader.

She was elected for a third term in 1987; thus, she became the first British prime minister in more than 150 years to win three consecutive elections. Support for Thatcher diminished toward the close of the decade. By 1990, she had lost the support of the Conservative Party, so she resigned as her party's leader and as prime minister. However, she remained as a member of the Parliament until 1992, and she became a member of the House of Lords.

Suggested Activities

Cartography: Draw maps of Great Britain.

History: Learn about the political structure of Great Britain over time. What role does the monarchy play? How are Britain's leaders selected? Answer these as well as other pertinent questions.

Definition: Margaret Thatcher was an ardent Conservative. Define the word *conservative*, and determine what it means politically.

Eighties Facts and Figures

Make a copy of the chart below for each pair of students. Direct them to use the information on this page as a comparison with a chart (page 87) they will complete about the current decade.

The United States in 1980	
Population:	226.5 million
Quart of milk:	$ .41
Loaf of bread:	$ .36
Dozen eggs:	$ .72
Pound of coffee:	$1.09
Minimum wage:	$3.10
Life Expectancy:	70.7 years (men), 78.1 years (women)

Popular Writers: Stephen King, Danielle Steele, Dr. Seuss, Alice Walker, Toni Morrison, Bill Cosby, Judy Blume, Lois Lowry, Salman Rushdie, Shel Silverstein

Popular Actors and Actresses: Drew Barrymore, Chevy Chase, John Belushi, Meryl Streep, Dustin Hoffman, Andy Kaufman, Molly Ringwald, Heather Locklear, Demi Moore, Andrew McCarthy, Bruce Willis, Bill Cosby, Harrison Ford, Cher, Meg Ryan, Joan Collins, Michael Landon, Kevin Kline, Glenn Close

Popular Recording Artists: Bruce Springsteen, U2, John Cougar Mellencamp, Cyndi Lauper, Prince, Michael Jackson, Whitney Houston, David Bowie, Tina Turner, Fleetwood Mac, Tom Petty and the Heartbreakers, Van Halen, Pat Benatar, B-52s, Jackson Browne, The Cars

Popular Movies: *Flashdance, Fame, The Breakfast Club, St. Elmo's Fire, Gandhi, Sophie's Choice, The Karate Kid, Ghostbusters, A Christmas Story, Back to the Future, Top Gun, Raiders of the Lost Arc, Poltergeist, Ferris Bueller's Day Off, E.T.: The Extra-terrestrial, Footloose, When Harry Met Sally, Bull Durham, The World According to Garp, The Big Chill*

Popular Songs: "Beat It," "Bette Davis Eyes," "What's Love Got to Do With It," "I Want to Dance with Somebody," "Footloose," "Flashdance (What a Feeling)," "Stop Draggin' My Heart Around," "Jump," "Let's Go Crazy," "Born in the U.S.A.," "Jack and Diane," "Modern Love," "Let's Hear It for the Boy," "Fame"

New Products: Cabbage Patch Kids, Trivial Pursuit, Rubik's Cube, Post-It Notes, *USA Today,* Nutrasweet, Teddy Ruxpin, B-2 bomber, IBM personal computer, blue corn chips

Sports Stars: Mary Lou Retton, Wayne Gretzsky, Florence Griffith Joyner, Mike Tyson, Larry Bird, Magic Johnson, Carl Lewis, Joe Montana, Jose Canseco, Bonnie Blair, Steffi Graf, Mike Schmidt, Rickey Henderson, Julius "Dr. J." Erving

Popular Television Shows: *The Wonder Years, Facts of Life, Family Ties, Knight Rider, Moonlighting, The Jeffersons, 21 Jump Street, Alf, Cheers, CHiPs, Miami Vice, The A-Team, The Golden Girls, Dallas, Dynasty, Magnum P.I., Hill Street Blues, Donahue, Quantum Leap, Star Trek: The Next*

       86

Comparing the Times

With a partner, fill in the blanks on this page about the current decade. Compare your answers with the information about the eighties (page 86).

Population: _____

Quart of milk: _____

Loaf of bread: _____

Dozen eggs: _____

Pound of coffee: _____

Minimum wage: _____

Life Expectancy: _____

Popular Writers:

Popular Actors and Actresses:

Popular Recording Artists:

Popular Movies:

Popular Songs:

New Products:

Sports Stars:

Popular Television Shows:

Famous Firsts

In the 1980s, the United States saw the first

. . . live debates in the Senate broadcast over television.

. . . IBM personal computer.

. . . compact disc.

. . . woman graduate from West Point Academy.

. . . woman (Mary Decker) to run the mile in less than 4.5 minutes.

. . . "mouse" and "pulldown menu" for personal computers.

. . . solar-cell power plant.

. . . long-distance, solar-powered airplane flight.

. . . solar-powered flight across the English Channel.

. . . nonstop flight around the world with no refueling.

. . . genetically engineered commercial product (insulin produced by bacteria).

. . . space shuttle flight.

. . . permanent artificial heart to be placed in a human patient.

. . . spacecraft to leave the solar system.

. . . artificially created chromosome.

. . . genes from an ancient species to be cloned.

. . . astronauts to fly in space without being tethered to a spaceship.

. . . photos of a planetary system around another "sun," Beta Pictoris.

. . . vaccine for humans made by genetic engineering.

. . . billionaire of the microcomputer industry (Bill Gates).

. . . scientifically produced vertebrate (a mouse) to receive a patent.

. . . B-2 "Stealth" bomber.

. . . DNA tests used as evidence in some criminal cases.

. . . lasers used to clear blocked arteries.

. . . holographic image on a credit card.

. . . blue corn chips.

. . . woman Supreme Court associate justice.

. . . American woman in space.

. . . black astronaut in space.

. . . private citizen in space.

. . . director of national drug control policy (William J. Bennett).

. . . movie to earn more than $700 million (*E.T.: The Extra-Terrestrial*).

. . . broadcast of MTV.

. . . inline skates.

1990 and Beyond

- The decade opened with the fall of the Union of Soviet Socialist Republics (U.S.S.R.), followed by restructuring and civil wars throughout the area. Mikhail Gorbachev, the Soviet leader who had been instrumental in bringing about the change, fell out of power and a new era, under the leadership of Boris Yeltsin and others, began.

- War tore apart the nation of Bosnia-Herzegovina, once a part of Yugoslavia, in the aftermath of the Soviet demise. Kosovo in Yugoslavia also saw ethnic war and international intervention.

- Women were on the rise in the United States. The nineties saw the first female attorney general, Janet Reno. Madeline Albright became the first female secretary of state. The position of first lady, the wife of the president, also saw an increased sphere of power and influence in Hillary Rodham Clinton.

- Citizens throughout the United States grieved over the bombing of the Alfred P. Murrah Federal Building in Oklahoma City, Oklahoma, in which 168 people were killed.

- Nelson Mandela, the former political prisoner, became the president of South Africa. Apartheid, the law of racial inequity and separation, ended.

- Hundreds of thousands of black men "marched" to Capitol Hill in Washington, D.C., in a show of solidarity and commitment to racial and family values. Promoters, calling for one million men to join in the march, named the event the Million Man March.

- Sports superstars of phenomenal prowess came to the forefront, including the young Tiger Woods who was instrumental in broadening the appeal of golf to millions of Americans. Also noteworthy were the women's gymnastics, swimming, volleyball, softball, and basketball teams of the United States in the 1996 Summer Olympics. Their record-breaking firsts—and gymnast Kerri Strug's act of courage—have become legendary.

- The Microsoft Company grew to be one of the most powerful in the world under the creative leadership of its founder, Bill Gates.

- Technology was at the forefront of industry, education, and home life. Everywhere around the world, people were "surfing the net," computing through CD-ROM, exploring virtual reality, and talking on the go via their cellular phones.

- Amid the Israeli-Palestinian peace talks, an assassin killed Prime Minister Yitzhak Rabin, the Israeli leader at the forefront of peace negotiations. In 1994, Rabin shared the Nobel Peace Prize with fellow Israeli Shimon Peres and Palestine Liberation Organization leader Yasir Arafat.

- Bill Clinton became the president of the decade with comfortable wins in the 1992 and 1996 elections. However, third-party candidacy was on the rise, largely through the leadership of Reform Party candidate Ross Perot. Clinton's second term, in particular, was marred by scandal.

- Little green men from Mars were not such an unlikely thing: evidence of life was found on the fourth planet.

- Rap music filled the airwaves while gang-related violence filled the streets. Several of the world's most successful rap stars were gunned down in gang activity, including Tupac Shakur and the Notorious B.I.G. Both were part of the rap movement known as gangsta rap.

Literature Connections

Literature Ideas: The following books can be used to supplement and enhance the study of the 1980s. They were either published in the decade or depict a segment of life from the time.

- *The Indian in the Cupboard* by Lynn Reid Banks (1980)
  One of the most popular children's books of the eighties, *The Indian in the Cupboard* tells the fantasy story of a boy and a magical cupboard that brings toys to life.

- *The Day They Came to Arrest the Book* by Nat Hentoff (1982)
  This story of censorship takes place in a high school circa 1980.

- *A Ring of Endless Light* by Madeleine L'Engle (1980)
  One of many books for young adults from the eighties that deals with mystical and even spiritual themes, this is a story of a girl's communion with dolphins.

- *Strider* by Beverly Cleary (1991)
  This poignant and popular story tells of a boy living a life common to many children in the eighties, being raised by single parents.

- *Journey* by Patricia MacLachlan (1991)
  Many of MacLachlan's books take place in this period of time. This story is regionally midwestern. It is the moving tale of a young boy's journey for his identity. He finds it through the loving help of his grandfather.

- *A Light in the Attic* by Shel Silverstein (1981)
  Silverstein's whimsical, funny, and sometimes touching poetry is enjoyed by people of all ages. Share several of his poems from this collection with your class.

- *1984* by George Orwell (1949)
  Although this book is difficult to understand and should only be attempted by mature students, it is worth noting as an interesting look into the future by an author of the 1940s. Use discretion.

Extensions: Use these ideas to enhance the literature your students read.

Read and Review: Read any of the books on this page and prepare a review to present the book to the class. Be sure to state a clear opinion about the book and support your ideas.

Let's Go to the Movies: After reading one of these books, create a movie poster advertising the "film version." Be sure to show a significant image that will demonstrate the theme of the movie. Also include the title. Add other touches as you choose.

Act It Out: After reading one of the novels, be prepared to be interviewed by the class as the main character of the book. One at a time, class members can take turns being the lead characters. Others in the class can ask questions about the character's life and experiences. The questions can refer to actual things stated in the book or they may require some creative thought in order to be answered.

Different Time: Take the main character from one of these novels and write a new version of his or her story, placing the character in a different decade of the twentieth century.

Writing Prompts

Writing Prompts Use these suggestions for journal writing or as daily writing exercises. Some research or discussion may be appropriate before assigning a particular topic.

- Imagine you are a fan at one of the two Live Aid concerts. Describe what you see and how you feel.

- You are standing atop the Berlin Wall on the day it is finally torn down. Describe the experience.

- You are part of the crowd watching the space shuttle *Challenger* takeoff for its tenth mission. Suddenly, it explodes in midair. Describe the scene as though it is happening now.

- Write a speech that might have been given by one of the major world leaders of the eighties.

- Write the storyboard for a music video to go along with one of your favorite songs.

- Write your ideas for putting an end to terrorism.

- Name a leader from the eighties whom you admire. Describe him or her and the reasons for your admiration.

- Imagine you are a child from 1888 who has been magically transported into a home in 1988. Write a story about what happens and what you experience.

- Imagine that your family has just gotten a VCR for the first time. Write an account of how you react and what you think of the new machine.

- You want to spike your hair with mousse and gel like you see in videos on the new music channel, MTV, and your mother will not allow you to do it. Write your conversation as you try to persuade her.

- You are a reporter covering the American hockey team at the 1980 Winter Olympics. Write your story.

- Jimmy Carter and Ronald Reagan are debating the issues in 1980. Write a conversation that Carter and Reagan could have had.

- You witness Florence Griffith Joyner's amazing success at the 1988 Olympic trials and games. Describe what you see.

- You are there when Ben Johnson's gold medal is taken away after he is discovered to have used anabolic steroids. Write an argument for or against this action.

- Imagine that you can design a new video game. Describe the game and how to play it.

- Jimmy Carter has just decreed that the U.S. will boycott the 1980 Summer Olympic Games. Write a letter to the president with your reaction.

- You watched Joe Montana lead the San Francisco 49ers through four championship seasons in the eighties. Describe a memorable play you saw.

Me in 1980

Imagine yourself at your age in 1980. Complete the following prompts, using what you imagine to fill in the blanks.

Where I live:
What my home is like:
What I do when I get up in the morning:
What a typical school day is like:
What I do for fun:
My chores:
How my family spends our evenings:

Buzzwords

New inventions, habits, lifestyles, and occupations cause people to invent new words. The ninth decade of the new century was no exception. Listed below are some of the words and phrases that came into popular use throughout the decade.

AIDS—This is an acronym for Acquired Immune Deficiency Syndrome, a condition caused by a virus that affects the immune system.

break dancing—This form of dance incorporates rippling movements of the body, unusual twisting of the limbs, and spinning on the back and head.

compact disc—Music and other audios are recorded on a laser disc, replacing vinyl records.

cross-training—This is the process of preparing oneself physically for different athletic skills or abilities at the same time.

fax—This shortened form of facsimile refers to an electronic reproduction of documents on paper, sent via the phone system.

focus group—This term refers to a group of individuals gathered by an organization in order to share their insights and opinions on a given topic or topics.

glasnost—This word means openness in Russian and is used to describe a political and social trend.

home shopping—Items available for purchase are presented on television. The shopper orders by telephone.

Iron Lady—This nickname was given to British Prime Minister Margaret Thatcher, denoting her stalwart type of leadership.

junk bond—This is a type of corporate bond (certificate of debt guaranteeing payment plus interest) having a high yield and a high risk.

linear thinking—This phrase describes a thought process that moves from point to point in a singular fashion, without deviance.

moonwalk—This dance step, in which the dancer appears to move forward while actually moving backward, was popularized by performer Michael Jackson.

music video—This is a brief movie visually depicting the content or sense of a corresponding song.

PC—This abbreviation originally referred to an IBM personal computer.

quality time—This term refers to time spent with one's children that is characterized by positive interaction.

Solidarity—This was the name given to the Polish labor organization.

space shuttle—This is the name given to a reusable spacecraft developed by NASA.

spin doctor—This term refers to an individual in charge of tailoring actual events regarding an individual, group, or organization to present a favorable image of the person, etc., to the public.

thirty-something—This term refers to someone in the age group of thirty to thirty-nine and was popularized by a television drama of the same name.

Valley girl—This phrase is used to describe a particular style of speech and attitude characteristic of the 1980s and associated with the San Fernando Valley of California.

VCR—This is the acronym for video-cassette recorder, a machine attached to a television that plays or records movies and shows.

VJ—This is a short form of video jockey, an announcer and host of music video broadcasts in the same style as disc jockeys of a radio station.

wannabee—This describes an individual who appears to "want to be" like another individual or group.

Yuppie—This term stands for "young urban professional," individuals whose lives revolve around professional careers and socio-economic advancement.

Software in the Classroom

More and more software is finding its way into the classroom. Many of the multimedia packages allow students to access photos, speeches, film clips, maps, and newspapers of various eras in history. Although a program may not be written specifically for the topic you are studying, existing software may be adapted for your purposes. To get maximum use from these programs and to learn how to keep up with technology, try some of the suggestions below.

Software

American Heritage: The History of the United States for Young People. Byron Press Multimedia

American History CD. Multi-Educator.

Chronicle of the 20th Century. Dorling Kindersley Ltd.

Compton's Encyclopedia of American History. McGraw Hill.

Compton's Interactive Encyclopedia. Compton's New Media, Inc.

The Cruncher. Microsoft Works.

Encarta (various editions). Microsoft Home.

Ideas That Changed the World. Ice Publishing.

Our Times: Multimedia Encyclopedia of the 20th Century (Vicarious Points of View Series 2.0). Scholastic.

Presidents: A Picture History of Our Nation. National Geographic.

Time Almanac. Compact Publishing (available through Broderbund, 800-922-9204).

TimeLiner. Tom Snyder Productions (800-342-0236).

Time Traveler CD! Orange Cherry.

Vital Links. Educational Resources (includes videodisc and audio cassette).

Where in America's Past Is Carmen Sandiego? Broderbund.

Using the Programs

After the initial excitement of using a new computer program wears off, you can still motivate students by letting them use the programs in different ways.

1. Print out a copy of a time line for the eighties for each group of students. Assign each group a different topic (for example, entertainment or politics). Direct the groups to research their topics and add text and pictures to their time line.

2. Let each pair of students choose a specific photo from the ninth decade of the twentieth century. Have them research the person or event and write a news story to go with it.

If you do not have enough computers in your classroom, hook your computer to a television screen for whole-class activities and let the students take turns typing. Keep a kitchen timer handy. For more ideas, see TCM 517 *Managing Technology in the Classroom* (Teacher Created Materials) or TCM 2457 *Managing Technology in the One-Computer Classroom.*

Internet

If you have access to the Internet, let the students search for related information. First ask the students to brainstorm a list of keywords or topics. Use a web browser like Alta Vista or Web Crawler to search for sites. Facts, pictures, and sound clips are only a click away. As an alternative, you may wish to preview sites and provide students with a list of URLs for access. See page 96 for Web sites.

Note: If the students will be searching, you may wish to install a filtering program, like SurfWatch from Spyglass, to limit access to objectionable material. Check with your Internet service provider.

Bibliography

Aaseng, Nathan. *You Are the President.* Oliver Press, Inc., 1994

Davis, Kenneth C. *Don't Know Much About History.* Crown Publishers, 1990

Denam, Cherry. *The History Puzzle: An Interactive Visual Timeline.* Turner Publishing, 1995

Duden, Jane. *Timelines.* Crestwood House, 1989

English, June. *Transportation: Automobiles to Zeppelins.* Scholastic, 1995

Felder, Deborah G. *The Kids' World Almanac of History.* Pharos Books, 1991

Grun, Bernard. *The Timetables of History.* Simon and Schuster, 1991

Hakim, Joy. *All the People.* Oxford University Press, 1995

Hopkinson, Christina. *The Usborne History of the Twentieth Century.* Usborne Publishing, 1993

Kranz, Rachel. *The Biographical Dictionary of Black Americans.* Facts on File, 1992

Napoli, Tony, ed. *Our Century: 1980–1990.* Gareth Stevens Publishing, 1993

The Oxford Children's Book of Famous People. Oxford University Press, 1994

Platt, Richard. *The Smithsonian Visual Timeline of Inventions.* Dorling Kindersley, 1994

Rubel, David. *The Scholastic Encyclopedia of the Presidents and Their Times.* Scholastic, 1994

————*The United States in the 20th Century.* Scholastic, 1995

Sharman, Margaret. *Take Ten Years: 1980s.* Steck-Vaughn, 1994

Skarmeas, Nancy. *First Ladies of the White House.* Ideals Publications, 1995

Smith, Carter. *Presidents in a Time of Change.* The Millbrook Press, 1993

Teacher Created Materials

#064 *Share the Olympic Dream*
#069 *Elections*
#1855 *20th Century Bulletin Board*
#2352 *20th Century: Inventions, Discoveries, and Highlights*
#2601 *20th Century Quiz Book*

Web Sites

The Ultimate 1980s Trivia Quiz and Other Fun Eighties Stuff

home.ptdprolog.net/~rkreider/eighties

This site is just as it sounds—a fun way to walk down memory lane in the eighties. The trivia centers around popular culture.

80s Popular Culture

ftp.southeast.net/~oct24/Songs_80s.htm

More trivia on popular culture.

Encyclopedia Americana: Presidents

gi.grolier.com/presidents/ea/bios/39pcart.html (for Carter)

gi.grolier.com/presidents/ea/bios/40preag.html (for Reagan)

gi.grolier.com/presidents/ea/bios/41pbush.html (for Bush)

These sites contain excellent encyclopedic biographies on each of the presidents of the eighties.

Timeline of Communications History 1980-1990

www.tec.spcomm.uiuc.edu/nosh/MGINFO/tsld009.htm

Here you will find a simple time line history of communications advancements during the eighties.

Media History Timeline

www.mediahistory.com/time/timeline.html

This site contains a time line overview of media advancements and inventions throughout time.

History Timelines

www.search-beat.com/history.htm

This is a central source for history links so browsers can focus in on a time or topic of interest.

Space Shuttle Program 1981-Present

208.240.91.104/timeline/tl_80.htm

An excellent source for studying the history of the space shuttle program.

Answer Key

page 25

1. B	11. C
2. R	12. B
3. C	13. C
4. R	14. B
5. C	15. C
6. B	16. B
7. R	17. R
8. C	18. R
9. R	19. R
10. R	20. C

page 31

1. 9
2. 79,388,000
3. 1,623
4. 541
5. 538 (1980 and 1984)
6. 98,359,000
7. 45%
8. 9%